YEADON'S REGISTER

of

L N E R

LOCOMOTIVES

Volume Thirty-One

**Class C6, C7, C8, C9, the
North Eastern Atlantics**

YEADON'S REGISTER OF L.N.E.R. LOCOMOTIVES - VOLUME 31

EDITOR'S NOTE & ACKNOWLEDGEMENTS

It was hoped that the former North British Railway Atlantics of LNER Class C10 and C11 could be accommodated within this volume but space considerations preclude their inclusion. However, what we do have is a superb presentation of the former North Eastern Atlantics comprising classes C6 to C9. It is because of the numerous illustrations, each one depicting a segment of the history of these engines, that space became too tight to include the C10 and C11 classes. Still to come of course are the other Atlantics of the Great Central, Great Northern and North British railways, the tank engines but until then we present the NER Atlantic tender engines.

The acknowledgements for each volume do not always mention the dozens of different photographers on whom WBY relied to help create this illustrated record. Most are no longer with us but their photographs continue to please an otherwise unforgiving audience.

Thanks for help and assistance in the production of this volume are due to numerous people and as usual Eric Fry heads the list for without his imput we would find it very difficult to go to press. However, besides EVF there are the typesetters and printers to whom we are grateful for the continuing 'quality' they produce.

Two thirds of the staff at the University Archive in Hull are new to their posts but already they have settled into being a helpful and friendly bunch; as for the other third, well its business as usual and the whole team make each visit a pleasure.

For Jean and Simon this is another volume to add to their bookshelf and we hope that they still believe in us to finish the job.

The next *Yeadon's Register of LNER Locomotives*, Volume 32, is a real miscellany of classes featuring the locomotives with the X classification, the Y2, Y4 to Y10 and the two examples under the letter Z.

Material contained within this volume has the following catalogue references:
DYE/1/17; DYE/1/18; DYE/1/87; DYE/2/2.

The Yeadon Collection is available for inspection and anyone who wishes to inspect it should contact:-
The Archivist
Brynmor Jones Library
University of Hull
Hull
HU6 7RX
Tel: 01482-465265
A catalogue of the Yeadon collection is available.

First published in the United Kingdom by
BOOK LAW PUBLICATIONS 2004 in association with CHALLENGER
382 Carlton Hill, Nottingham, NG4 1JA.
Printed and bound by The Amadeus Press, Cleckheaton, West Yorkshire.

INTRODUCTION

C6

At the dawn of the twentieth century the East Coast Main Line trains between London and Edinburgh had become so heavy, it was necessary for the two companies responsible for their haulage to invest in stronger motive power. The Great Northern, which took care of these trains between London and York had, in 1902, brought out a large Atlantic type locomotive which was a bigger version of the 'Klondyke' Atlantic introduced onto the GNR by Ivatt in 1898 (*see also* Vol.13). Eventually ninety-four of the very capable 'Large Atlantics' would form the backbone of the GN express passenger motive power pool for the ECML trains until after Grouping. The North Eastern Railway, which hauled the ECML trains between York and Edinburgh had decided to put their money into two classes of the 4-6-0 type. However, these six-coupled engines, one class having 6ft 1¼in. coupled wheels (LNER B13) and the other with 6ft 8¼in. wheels (LNER B14), did not have the necessary power to cope with the heavy trains. The North Eastern CME of the time, Wilson Worsdell, recognised the problem with the 4-6-0's and noting that the GNR Atlantics seemed to handle the ECML trains with relative ease, he decided that a 4-4-2 design would be the answer for the NER. To back up his case further, he had on a recent visit to the Pennsylvania Railroad in the United States, observed the way in which their Atlantic type engines handled the railroad's express passenger traffic.

In November 1903 the result of Worsdell's inspiration came out of Gateshead works in the shape of No.532, the first of ten such two-cylinder engines to come off the Tyneside production line during the next twelve months. These ten, numbered somewhat haphazardly in order of building as 532, 649, 784, 295, 1680, 742, 1753, 1776, 1792 and 1794, were classified V on the NER (LNER Class C6). During 1910 another ten, numbered 696 to 705, were built at Darlington and, although differing in minor details from the Gateshead engines, they became NER Class V/09; the last two digits actually signifying that the construction drawings for them were prepared in 1909.

The Atlantics promised to be everything that the NER required for the ECML expresses and, like their GN predecessors, worked the heavy Scottish services until Grouping but continued on main line work until the late 1930's. In common with the GN engines, the NER Atlantics had 5ft 6in. diameter boilers but these were not equipped with a wide firebox. The same size of boiler was to be used on the later Raven three cylinder Atlantics (NER Class Z - LNER Class C7) and in latter years these boilers were often inter-changed between the classes.

The first ten boilers built in 1903-4 at Gateshead for Class V did not carry superheaters and were scrapped between 1912 and 1919. Three spare boilers (one in 1906 and two in 1909) were also built at Gateshead for the class. These three and the ten built at Darlington in 1910 for the V/09 series Atlantics were also saturated at first, but all subsequently received Schmidt pattern superheaters and were cut-up between 1921 and 1927. After conversion some of the 1910-built boilers found their way onto Class C7. All subsequent boilers built at Darlington were used indiscriminately on both C6 and C7 classes. Those built from December 1931 had Robinson superheaters and the last new Diagram 48 boilers were made in November 1936.

A peculiarity on Class C6 was the adoption in 1926 of the twin GER type anti-vacuum valves positioned behind the chimney for the superheater protection, the only known use of this Stratford feature on other than GE design locomotives. All the C6's received these valves and except for No.705 from 1935 to 1940, kept them to withdrawal. Class C7, although using the same boiler design, always had the simple Gresley anti-vacuum valve.

Originally fitted with the Westinghouse brake for engine and train, the class was also equipped with vacuum ejectors for alternative train braking. To bring the C6 class in line with the Unification of Brakes Programme of 1928, the vacuum brake became the main braking for the train and the planned installation of steam braking was to be used for engine braking thus rendering the Westinghouse gear redundant. However, with finances critical in the early 1930's, the LNER converted just six of the C6 class to steam braking for the engine; the other fourteen keeping the Westinghouse brakes to withdrawal but with the air lines suitably capped off at the train connections.

Of the twenty engines comprising Class C6, the last fifteen had been built with steam operated reversing gear whilst the first five were equipped with the simpler screw reverse gear. This latter equipment was to replace the steam operated gear during the 1930's and by April 1939 all the class had screw reverse fitted.

Being amongst the best express motive power the North Eastern possessed, the C6 shared the bulk of the ECML express passenger train haulage between York and Edinburgh with their 3-cylinder counterparts the C7's. Even at Grouping they were still regarded as extremely capable for the job and they remained at sheds adjacent to the main line as they had done since introduction. The Newcastle area had the largest allocation with twelve or thirteen shared between Gateshead and Heaton; besides their ECML C6 diagrams, these sheds also provided C6's for the Carlisle line trains. York had four C6's and to the north, Tweedmouth had three. Things remained much the same even when the Raven and, later, the Gresley Pacifics began to take on more of the express passenger trains in the North Eastern Area of the LNER. However, in 1928 the first moves away from the four sheds mentioned came into effect and four C6's were sent to Darlington to act as main line pilots, ready for use in the event of Pacific failure on the main line. They also began to take on more express goods work but only within the area bounded by their former stomping ground between Edinburgh and York. No.532 was used, during the mid-1920's, by the Bridge Testing Committee and got as far as the former Great Eastern area at Broxbourne, but from 1924 the C6's began to visit King's Cross. Prior to Grouping NER Atlantics were fairly rare in London but from 1924 they became regular visitors, the C7's more so than the C6's.

By 1930 the Tweedmouth allocation was changed for C7's and once again the C6's were shared between four sheds. From 1938 the C6's began in infiltrate new areas when much of their main line work was taken over by V2's and K3's. Leeds Neville Hill shed gained a couple in that year whilst Scarborough got six in the summer of 1939 and Bridlington also acquired six, including the two Leeds engines, at the same time. Darlington had the other eight. The two coastal sheds found little work for them in the months leading up to war and they spent much of their time in periods of storage. Once hostilities started the C6's returned to the main line in 1940 and spent the next three years of war working from York, Darlington, Gateshead and Heaton sheds on passenger, parcels and 'fast' goods trains. In March 1943, after the first withdrawal earlier in the year, the class was once again subject to an allocation reshuffle which was basically to be their last. As a result of this Gateshead, which had a long association with the class, ended up with five but the other fourteen went to sheds which had seen little if anything of their type before. Hull Dairycoates got two; the former Hull & Barnsley shed at Cudworth got two whilst the rest went to another ex H&B shed - Hull Springhead. Except for the Gateshead engines, the move did not prove a good omen for the class as they were relegated to goods work which was hardly suitable for these engines.

Being express passenger engines, this class was accorded the lined green livery on both the North Eastern and the LNER although during their latter working days the engines, like all green liveried LNER engines, they started to wear plain black paint from the middle years of WW2. Of the eight engines scrapped in 1943-44, six were withdrawn before they succumbed to black livery and another, No.784 which survived the conflict, actually kept its green livery and original LNER lettering (though renumbered to 2931) to its late 1947 withdrawal.

Being of NER origin, these engines carried their original numbers through Grouping into the LNER period and up to the Thompson renumbering scheme of the 1940's. However, there were a few cases where an area suffix was attached during the early years of the LNER. When the Thompson renumbering was drawn up in July 1943, the class had already lost one member to the scrapyard so that the new scheme issued the number block 2930 to 2948 to take account of the nineteen survivors in the July 1943 census. When the number groups were actually published in December of that year, a further C6 had been condemned and this engine No.649 was, by some stroke of fortune, to have taken up the number 2930. Therefore the published list was revised as 2931 to 2948. But, it was a few years between the December 1943 publishing date and the actual implementation in 1946 with the result that only seven C6's got their new numbers. Although two engines survived to become BR property, neither of those lasted long enough to gain British Railways numbers both were condemned within three months of nationalisation.

C7

The NER were obviously pleased with their twenty Worsdell Atlantics and in 1910 required another dozen at least. In that same year the office of Chief Mechanical Engineer had changed when Wilson Worsdell retired early and Vincent Raven had stepped into his shoes. With the Atlantic requirement on the order books, the new CME saw an opportunity to introduce 3-cylinder propulsion to NER express passenger engines and therefrom the North Eastern Class Z was born of which no less than fifty examples would be built between 1911 and 1918.

Due to the NER's own workshops being very busy in 1910, the company was required to order from outside contractors which in this case was the North British Loco. Co. in Glasgow. NBL supplied the first twenty, all in 1911 and from two orders of ten each. These were numbered 706, 709, 710, 714, and 716 to 721; 722, 727, 728, 729, and 732 to 737. The next batch of 'Z's came from Darlington in 1914 in the shape of ten engines numbered 2163 to 2172. These in turn were followed by twenty more all built at Darlington between 1914 and 1918 and numbered consecutively 2193 to 2212. The very last Z class engine, No.2212 emerged from Darlington exactly one year after the previous Z class, No.2211, had gone into traffic. The reason

for the extended period between the penultimate and last engine of the class appearing was because No.2212 had been fitted with 'Uniflow' cylinders, the NER's second attempt at improving the passage of steam through a locomotive's valves and cylinders. Five years previously one of the North Eastern's 4-6-0's, No.825 of Class S2, had also been fitted from new with 'Uniflow' cylinders (see Volume 17) and its appearance was far from pleasing whereas that of the Atlantic was quite acceptable.

Apart from No.2212, the Z class Atlantics were very similar to the V and V/09 class engines; same size boilers; same size leading, driving, trailing and tender wheels; very similar tractive effort and, outwardly similar. Both had Stephenson motion but with different size piston valves. However, the Raven engines had three instead of two cylinders and these were of course of smaller diameter and stroke.

Of the twenty built in 1911 by the NBL, the first ten came with saturated boilers whilst the next ten arrived with boilers equipped with the Schmidt type superheater. The ten saturated boilers were converted to carry Schmidt superheaters during 1914-15. Apart from these ten boilers originally without superheaters (used as such on Class C7), all other boilers, original and replacement, were used interchangeably on C7 and C6. As mentioned above, until 1931 Schmidt superheaters were standard. Thereafter the Robinson pattern was used on the twenty-seven replacements built up to 1936. Actually twenty-eight were constructed during this period but one was given a Schmidt superheater (in March 1934) to use up the existing stock. The Diagram 48 type boiler was not amongst those redesigned at this time for certain other former NER classes of engine.

In 1931 Nos.727 and 2171 were rebuilt with booster engines and these then were reclassified C9.

During the 1920's and 30's certain members of the class were subject to feed water heating experiments but none were satisfactory enough for general adoption on C7 class. No.2163 had the Dabeg type and this was removed in January 1937. The ACFI apparatus, which saw extensive use on the ex GER 4-6-0 engines of Class B12, was more satisfactory and C7 Nos.728 and 2206 kept their gear until wartime conditions brought about the removal of all 'gadgets' from LNER locomotives; No.2206 lost its ACFI equipment in June 1941 and No.728 in March 1942.

Another development which affected C7 class was the introduction of Lentz Poppet Valves. In 1933 No.732 was rebuilt quite extensively with the above mentioned valves. To accommodate the Lentz gear, the front end of the engine was made longer, a new bogie with smaller wheels was fitted and new larger cylinders replaced the originals. No.732 was designated Class Part 2 as a result of the modifications and it was joined in 1936 by the 'Uniflow' engine, No.2212 when it too got the Lentz gear, albeit an improved version, new cylinders and the necessary rebuilding to fit it all in. All the others in the class became Part 1 and no others were changed to the Lentz rotary type motion.

In 1921 No.2202 was changed from coal to oil firing and then ran with a modified tender holding 1240 gallons of fuel-oil in a tank fitted into the coal space of its tender. In the following year the Scarab fuel-oil system was removed from the engine and the coal space in the tender returned to its original usage.

Like their C6 counterparts, the C7's spent their NER days on main line express work between York and Edinburgh. The majority were shedded on Tyneside, whilst York had thirteen, Neville Hill three for Liverpool-Newcastle services, and Haymarket had four up to Grouping. In 1923 the latter shed lost one of its C7's whilst the remaining three, now under LNER ownership were used on duties which had hitherto been

No.532 was built in November 1903 at Gateshead. It was without a windjabber on the chimney and with a cab roof pitched much too low which looked wrong and, was quickly proved wrong. Note the tender has only three open coal rails and that the smokebox is the waisted pattern and not mounted on a saddle.

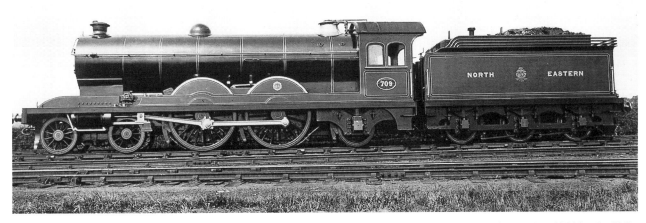

Ten engines, Nos.706, 709, 710, 714, 716, 717, 718, 719, 720 and 721, were built between July and September 1911 by the N.B. Loco. Co. without superheaters, for direct comparison with another ten built with superheaters.

One four cylinder Smith compound, No.730 was built in April 1906 with Stephenson motion to the valves. A reducing valve on the side of the smokebox enabled the engine to be worked as either a simple, semi-compound or full compound. In March 1915 a new (superheated) boiler was put on and this was retained to the engines January 1935 withdrawal.

unfamiliar to them such as the Edinburgh to Glasgow (Queen St) stopping trains.

Those engines attached to the ECML sheds in England continued to use them on main line duties between York and Edinburgh but southwards, Grantham became a regular destination for the Gateshead engines after Grouping. Prior to 1923 King's Cross saw the occasional C7 but from 1924 they became regular visitors on excursions and special trains. As the Gresley Pacifics especially began to take over the bulk of the ECML passenger services, the C7's were put on to other routes such as the Carlisle road from Newcastle, and the Hull and Scarborough routes from York and not just on passenger work either as they were quite at home on express goods trains, though they remained allocated to the ECML sheds.

At the beginning of WW2, York had no less than twenty-six of the C7's allocated. Gateshead and Heaton still had fourteen between them and Neville Hill had got back three in the previous year. Tweedmouth also had three but Haymarket was down to just one whilst St Margarets likewise had a sole example, its first exNER Atlantic. Another shed to gain its first NER Atlantic was the tiny establishment at Alston where No.2211 spent six months in store during 1940 apparently evacuated from Heaton; it went to Gateshead in the November. Besides passenger and fast goods work, the C7's began to take on an increasing number of slow goods services because of the wartime demands on motive power but their time in main line service was nearly finished and in the massive motive power shake-up of March 1943 their 'cards were marked.' Following the C6's, no less than twenty-two of the class were sent to Dairycoates, a shed regarded by many as something of an elephant graveyard for locomotives and indeed it was. In that same year withdrawals started when two of the class went for scrap. The following year ten more C7's ended up in Darlington scrapyard, and so the withdrawals went on. Whilst at Hull the C7's were used on any work that could be found for them be it passenger trains to Leeds or trip pilots hauling wagons between the numerous siding groups then to be found in and around the city. Scarborough was another shed which received a batch of the Atlantics but they were not sent there until towards the end of hostilities in Europe and by then they were somewhat run down but Scarborough shed managed to get the best out of them and used them on passenger turns to Hull, Leeds and York. In the last year of the LNER the C7's were distributed amongst just three sheds; Dairycoates, Darlington and Scarborough, the latter shed having the bulk of them.

To help the LNER Directors choose Group liveries, Darlington turned out No.2169 on the 25th January 1923 in North Eastern Railway green with large brass numberplate but no armorial on the splasher. The tender carried 6in. L.&N.E.R. over 12in. numbers. On 19th February 1923, No.2207 appeared in GNR green with a small numberplate on the cab but with the tender in the same style as 2169. Both these had 6in. numbers at the front. No.2195 (24th April 1923) was first in this style followed from Darlington by 2198 (28th April), 722 (30th April), 2167 (15th May), 2210 (18th May), 706 (30th May) and 714 (31st May) and from Gateshead 2197 (16th May); all had 4½in. numbers at the front. The full points were soon dropped and the lettering became standard at 7½in. size. No.2200 was the first in that style, ex Darlington 20th June 1923. Before the end of summer the ampersand had also been dropped.

When the Thompson renumbering scheme was drawn up the fifty C7's had been reduced in number by two, which had been rebuilt by Gresley to Class C9 (*see* later). The survivors were allocated numbers 2950 to 2997 but by 1946 when the

renumbering got under way, only half of the class received their new numbers and of these, fourteen were allocated BR numbers with the addition of 60,000 but none lasted long enough to get them.

The first withdrawal was in August 1943 when No.2170 was condemned. By then the class was somewhat worn-out and scrapping began in earnest as hostilities came to an end. The fourteen that survived into 1948 had all gone by the end of that year, No.2970 (ex2164) of Dairycoates being the last to go in December and when it was cut up in the first month of 1949 Class C7 was extinct.

C8

The two NER Class 4CC which became LNER Class C8 were built in 1906 under Wilson Worsdell's reign as CME. The actual design of the locomotives was the responsibility of W.M.Smith, the company's Chief Draughtsman and the two compound Atlantics would not have been the sole members of their class had not a problem with design royalties, after Smith's untimely death, caused the NER to shy away from the expense that would have been involved.

The engines, numbered 730 and 731, had Belpaire firebox boilers feeding steam to two high pressure and two low pressure cylinders via just two sets of valves (Smith's design). No.730 had Stephenson motion whilst No.731 had Walschaerts. Superheated boilers using the Schmidt equipment, which further enhanced their performance, were not fitted until 1915 and in the event they each got only those boilers; the one-off nature of them precluded any new ones being constructed during the cash starved 1930's when renewal became necessary.

Both engines carried a Westinghouse brake and a vacuum ejector, the latter for alternative train braking and they both had dual-braked tenders which were not standard to North Eastern practice. Between the two engines there were a number of detail differences and these are highlighted in the captions and tables.

The two compounds were based at Gateshead from their introduction and worked express passenger trains to both Edinburgh and York during virtually the whole of the NER period. There were a couple of exceptions to this however. In 1908 Nos.730 and 731 worked the Waverley route whilst on loan to the North British Railway for comparison trials with the NB Atlantics. Up until the First World War both engines took part in numerous tests on the main line, clocking up some impressive performances just as they did in everyday usage up to Grouping. With the arrival of Gresley A1's at Gateshead in late 1924, the two C8's were put onto less demanding express duties but when the A3's reached there in 1930, they were virtually redundant and spent time in store. In 1931 they went on loan to Hull Botanic Gardens to work the Hull-Sheffield expresses but that sojourn only lasted for a few weeks. In November 1933 both were sent across the river to Heaton shed where No.730 was to spend its last year of life. No.731 did even less time at that shed and after only a couple of weeks it went to Darlington works for overhaul only to be withdrawn.

Both engines wore passenger lined green livery throughout their lives, No.731 gaining the LNER version with a D suffix in 1923 whilst No.730 kept its NER livery until 1925. Although No.730 had its number moved from tender to cab in 1930, No.731 kept its number on the tender through to withdrawal in 1933.

Obviously, their non-standard design, which although successful, was not to be tolerated and as soon as their boilers wore out the engines were withdrawn; No.731 in December 1933 and No.730 in January 1935.

C9

Class C9 was created by Gresley on the rebuilding of two C7 Atlantic into booster fitted engines in 1931. The two engines chosen were Nos.727 and 2171, both of which had arrived for repair at Darlington in early 1931.

The plan to fit booster engines to the exNER Atlantics was drawn up in 1927 as a result of tests carried out with similar equipment on former GNR C1 No.4419 from 1924 to 1927. Although the booster was found to be a useful tool when required, it was necessary to refine it further to do away with the rough riding and excessive axle loading associated with its fitting. By 1927 it was found that an articulated tender with a booster bogie situated beneath it and the locomotive cab would partly solve the riding deficiency and get rid of the axle loading problem. It was also found that a larger boiler would be needed to produce the required amount of steam. The boiler produced for the C9's was the Diagram 104 which had a sloping back and throat plates as per Doncaster designs; a Robinson superheater was fitted as standard.

A number of design changes to the booster layout were made by Darlington drawing office in conjunction with J.Stone & Co., the manufacturer of the booster engine, and several years passed before the whole ensemble was got together at Darlington ready for the conversion of the two C7's. In the event it took nearly the whole of 1931 before Nos.727 and 731 emerged for road trials in November and December respectively.

After the initial trials in the Darlington area with dynamometer car attached, No.727 still in under coat, was allowed to work north to Scotland and back. It then re-entered Darlington for final adjustments and to have fully lined green paint applied, ready for traffic.

From the outset these engines were doomed as there were insufficient crews able to handle the booster properly and the exNER Atlantics were no longer required to work the heavy ECML expresses any more because of the influx of Gresley Pacifics. However, the booster on No.2171 gave trouble for much of the time and the engine spent long periods in the shops or out on the road with the booster detached. Modifications of one form or another took place to try and eradicate the 'teething' problems. No.727 on the other hand had a relatively trouble free existence compared to the other C9. In December 1936 the booster was removed from No.2171 and two months later No.727 also had its booster equipment removed, though the articulated arrangement remained.

When rebuilt the engines lost the Westinghouse brake and got steam brake for the engine with vacuum brakes for the train.

The original tenders attached to these engines when Class C7, went instead to Q6 engines. Two new tenders were built to suit the booster bogie. Above the running plate these tenders had straight side sheets similar to standard LNER tenders of the period but below the running plate they had only four fixed wheels, the space normally occupied by the forward set of wheels being used instead to accommodate half of the booster bogie.

The C9's were allocated to Gateshead to work fast passenger, and goods trains to Edinburgh and York. Occasionally they would work the crack expresses when double-headed with a C7. The booster engine, though being problematical on No.2171, worked well on No.727 and it could be said that the booster experience was something of a success but it had come twenty years too late and had cost more money than originally budgeted for. In 1939 both ended up at Tweedmouth as main line pilots and after a year there moved south to Heaton for similar duties. In April 1942 No.2171 was withdrawn for scrap and in the following January No.727 was also condemned. Neither engine had figured in Thompson's renumbering scheme being withdrawn just too early.

The tenders survived and after rebuilding to a normal six-wheel outline, and a period in storage, ended up serving Thompson B1 engines to the end of their days.

Using the frames, cylinders, motion, coupled wheels and bogie wheels of No.727, a complete rebuild was made as a proper trial of what help a booster could be. A new boiler, with Robinson superheater, was provided and an exhaust steam injector was fitted. A booster bogie had a new tender articulated to it. A new 5in. wider cab of D49 design was put on, but at first did not have sight screens as shown in this view. No.727, after trials in shop grey, was painted green and went back into traffic on 23rd December 1931. Lifting holes had been put in the frames at the front.

The remaining nine engines of the order, Nos.649, 784, 295, 742, 1680, 1753, 1776, 1792, and 1794 were built from December 1903 to October 1904 and all had a cab roof at a more acceptable height. No.532 was so altered in December 1903. From 1909 the tender had an extra rail around the coal space and the rails were plated on the inside. Between April 1915 and November 1919 all ten were superheated and then got a circular smokebox, some $9\frac{1}{4}$ in. longer.

Ten more engines, Nos.696 to 705, were built at Darlington from May to September 1910. These had strengthened frames at the front end and a modified splasher arrangement. The smokebox was circular and on a saddle but superheaters were not put in until April 1914 (704) to March 1920 (697).

CLASS C 6

532

Gateshead 13.03.

To traffic 11/1903.

REPAIRS:
???. ?/?—?/9/06.**G.**
???. ?/?—?/3/11.**G.**
???. ?/?—?/4/15.**G.**
Ghd. 9—11/4/23.**L.**
Ghd. 20/5—28/8/24.**G.**
Dar. 6/10/25—25/1/26.**G.**
Dar. 3—24/6/26.**L.**
Dar. 17/11/27—24/2/28.**G.**
Anti-vacuum valves fitted.
Dar. 29/4—16/7/30.**G.**
Dar. 25/2—30/3/31.**N/C.**
Dar. 19/5—17/8/32.**G.**
Westinghouse to Steam brake.
Dar. 28/5—5/7/34.**G.**
Dar. 12/8/35.*Weigh.*
Dar. 23/2—15/4/37.**G.**
Dar. 19/10—10/12/37.**H.**
Dar. 22/3—3/6/38.**L.**
Dar. 3/11/38—6/1/39.**L.**
Dar. 16/9—5/10/39.**N/C.**
Dar. 15/8—22/10/40.**G.**
Dar. 18/12/40—28/1/41.**H.**
Dar. 5/5/42—13/7/42.**L.**
Dar. 12/1/43. *Not repaired.*

BOILERS:
G358.
G532 *(new)* ?/9/06.
G422 *(ex1776)* ?/3/11.
D377 *(new; sup)* ?/4/15.
2057 *(new)* 24/2/28.
D1412 *(ex742)* 5/7/34.
D1460 *(exC7 709)* 15/4/37.
2422 *(exC7 2203)* 22/10/40.

SHEDS:
Heaton.
York 9/2/25.
Scarborough 23/6/39.
York 11/3/40.

CONDEMNED: 30/1/43.
Cut up at Darlington.

649

Gateshead 14.03.

To traffic 12/1903.

REPAIRS:
???. ?/?—?/8/08.**G.**
???. ?/?—?/7/10.**G.**

???. ?/?—?/7/15.**G.**
Ghd. 19/12/23—14/3/24.**G.**
Ghd. 18—27/11/24.**L.**
Ghd. 20/3—2/6/25.**G.**
Ghd. 14—15/7/26.**N/C.**
Ghd. 27/1—22/2/27.**L.**
Ghd. 26/1—5/5/28.**G.**
Anti-vacuum valves fitted.
Ghd. 21—27/3/29.**L.**
Ghd. 12—27/9/29.**L.**
Ghd. 16/2—30/3/31.**G.**
Dar. 17/11/31—13/1/32.**H.**
Ghd. 27—29/7/32.**N/C.**
Dar. 16/3—6/4/33.**H.**
Dar. 19/6—14/8/34.**G.**
Dar. 31/10—27/12/35.**H.**
Dar. 16/11/37—7/2/38.**G.**
Dar. 24/3—12/7/41.**G.**
Dar. 26/5—26/6/42.**N/C.**
Dar. 24/11—22/12/42.**N/C.**
Dar. 15—29/1/43.**L.**
Dar. 7/7/43. *Not repaired.*

BOILERS:
G363.
G358 *(ex295)* ?/8/08.
G424 *(ex1794)* ?/7/10.
D2046 *(ex705; sup)* ?/7/15.
D1598 *(new)* 14/3/24.
D1637 *(exC7 2193)* 30/3/31.
D1586 *(exC7 2198)* 6/4/33.
2417 *(exC7 736)* 14/8/34.
D1598 *(ex698)* 7/2/38.

SHEDS:
Heaton.
York 4/7/38.
Scarborough 5/6/39.
York 11/3/40.
Heaton 7/12/40.
Hull Springhead 28/3/43.

CONDEMNED: 17/8/43.
Cut up at Darlington.

784

Gateshead 11.

To traffic 12/1903.

REPAIRS:
???. ?/?—?/12/08.**G.**
???. ?/?—?/12/13.**G.**
???. ?/?—?/3/19.**G.**
???. ?/?—22/8/22.**G.**
Ghd. 27/12/22—31/1/23.**L.**
Ghd. 20/11/24—4/3/25.**G.**
Ghd. 24/12/25—9/2/26.**L.**
Ghd. 14—15/6/27.**N/C.**

Ghd. 7/9—28/12/27.**G.**
Anti-vacuum valves fitted.
Ghd. 25/5—7/6/28.**L.**
Ghd. 26/10—28/11/28.**L.**
Ghd. 4/11—20/12/29.**G.**
Ghd. 12/5—10/7/31.**G.**
Dar. 17—21/9/34.
Tender change.
Dar. 30/1—19/3/35.**G.**
Dar. 2/9—14/10/36.**L.**
Dar. 16/2—27/4/38.**G.**
Dar. 13/1—21/2/39.**H.**
Dar. 16/6—9/8/41.**G.**
Dar. 7/11/47. *Not repaired.*

BOILERS:
G371.
G363 *(ex649)* ?/12/08.
G418 *(ex1792)* ?/12/13.
D804 *(new; sup)* ?/3/19.
D1456 *(exC7 2195)* 19/3/35.
D1662 *(exC7 2170)* 27/4/38.
2158 *(ex1794)* 9/8/41

SHEDS:
Heaton.
York 31/8/38.
Bridlington 12/6/39.
Heaton 2/11/40.
Gateshead 28/3/43.

RENUMBERED:
2931 24/11/46.

CONDEMNED: 15/11/47.
Cut up at Darlington.

295

Gateshead 12.

To traffic 6/1904.

REPAIRS:
???. ?/?—?/6/07.**G.**
???. ?/?—?/5/08.**G.**
???. ?/?—?/3/09.**G.**
???. ?/?—?/1/12.**G.**
???. ?/?—?/9/18.**G.**
Ghd. 29/11/22—21/3/23.**G.**
Ghd. 28/2—9/5/24.**L.**
Ghd. 30/6—5/7/24.**L.**
Ghd. 10—24/12/25.**L.**
Ghd. 13/4—28/5/26.**L.**
Ghd. 5/1—5/5/27.**G.**
Anti-vacuum valves fitted.
Ghd. 23/5—9/6/27.**L.**
Ghd. 9—17/8/27.**L.**
Ghd. 24/4—8/6/28.**L.**
Ghd. 16/12/29—17/2/30.**G.**

Dar. 20/10—25/11/30.**L.**
???. 31/12/30—9/1/31.**L.**
Ghd. 2—21/7/31.**L.**
Westinghouse to Steam brake.
???. 20—26/1/32.**N/C.**
Ghd. 10/5—29/6/32.**G.**
???. 4—28/5/34.
Tender repair.
Dar. 26/9—5/11/34.**L.**
New smokebox fitted.
Dar. 27/3—7/6/35.**G.**
???. 15/9—26/10/36.
Tender repair.
Dar. 26/1—19/3/37.**G.**
Dar. 16/1—27/2/39.**L.**
Dar. 1—30/7/40.**G.**
Dar. 16/12/40—6/2/41.**H.**
Dar. 4/8—5/9/41.**L.**
After collision.
Dar. 19/11—24/12/41.**H.**
Dar. 11/3/44. *Not repaired.*

BOILERS:
G418.
G358 *(ex532)* ?/6/07.
G418 *(ex spare)* ?/5/08.
G371 *(ex784)* ?/3/09.
G421 *(ex spare)* ?/1/12.
D781 *(new; sup)* ?/9/18.
D1799 *(exC7 734)* 29/6/32.
2305 *(ex696)* 7/6/35.
D1615 *(exC7 2166)* 19/3/37.
2577 *(ex1753)* 30/7/40.

SHEDS:
Gateshead.
Tweedmouth ?/6/24.
Gateshead 9/6/30.
Darlington 22/3/38.
Hull Springhead 28/3/43.

RENUMBERED:
Allocated **2932**.

CONDEMNED: 23/3/44.
Cut up at Darlington.

742

Gateshead 13.

To traffic 6/1904.

REPAIRS:
???. ?/?—?/2/10.**G.**
???. ?/?—?/6/17.**G.**
Ghd. ?/?—31/8/22.**G.**
Ghd. 7—19/5/24.**L.**
Ghd. 8/7—30/9/24.**G.**
Ghd. 12/10—9/11/25.**G.**

(above) Until 1931 all the superheaters on this class were of the Schmidt type and the boilers had three handholes to the firebox on the right hand side for washing out purposes.

(left) On the left-hand side these boilers had only two hand holes.

Boilers built from December 1931 had the Robinson superheater, except for one built in March 1934 to use up the available Schmidt material. These boilers were fitted with five washout plugs instead of the three handholes on the right hand side, but the odd boiler had the hand holes - *see* page 24, bottom.

(above) **The Robinson superheated boilers also had five washout plugs instead of two handholes on the left-hand side. Six of the C6, Nos.698, 699, 702, 704, 784 and 1792 were never fitted with a Robinson type superheater.**

(right) **For superheater element protection, a handwheel-controlled steam-circulating valve was mounted on the left-hand side of the smokebox.**

Beginning with No.699 in December 1926, the simpler anti-vacuum valve was used. Curiously, for a North Eastern class, one was put at each end of the header and the GE variant was used, solely on C6 class.

742 cont./
Dar. 13/1—27/5/27.**G.**
Anti-vacuum valves fitted.
Ghd. 11—21/2/28.**L.**
Ghd. 21—28/3/28.**L.**
Ghd. 12—21/12/28.**L.**
Ghd. 18/10—21/12/29.**G.**
Ghd. 7—27/1/30.**N/C.**
Ghd. 13—28/5/30.**L.**
Ghd. 7—19/5/31.**L.**
Ghd. 3—13/7/31.**N/C.**
Ghd. 20/9—2/11/32.**L.**
Dar. 2/3—21/4/34.**G.**
Dar. 4/3—17/7/35.**H.**
Dar. 13/10—9/12/36.**G.**
Screw reverse fitted.
Dar. 7/9—10/1/38.**H.**
Dar. 22/2—27/3/40.**G.**
Dar. 13—31/1/42.**L.**
Dar. 3—23/3/42.**L.**
Dar. 16/12/42—9/3/43.**G.**
Dar. 6/11—15/12/45.**L.**
Dar. 2/9—5/10/46.**G.**
Dar. 19/2/48. *Not repaired.*

BOILERS:
 G420.
 G821 *(new)* ?/2/10.
 G532 *(ex spare;sup)* ?/6/17.
D1412 *(new)* 31/8/22.
 2056 *(exC7 735)* 21/4/34.
D1497 *(exC7 717)* 9/12/36.
 2275 *(ex698)* 27/3/40.
 2420 *(ex1753)* 9/3/43.
 2418 *(ex700)* 5/10/46.

SHEDS:
Heaton.
York 28/8/38.
Bridlington 12/6/39.
Heaton 2/11/40.
Hull Springhead 28/3/43.
Hull Dairycoates 13/5/44.

RENUMBERED:
2933 5/10/46.

CONDEMNED: 6/3/48.
Cut up at Darlington.

___

1680

Gateshead 14.

To traffic 6/1904.

REPAIRS:
???. ?/?—?/12/10.**G.**
???. ?/?—?/12/12.**G.**
???. ?/?—?/11/19.**G.**
???. ?/?—18/8/22.**G.**
Ghd. 11/3—12/6/24.**G.**
Dar. 20/10/25—10/2/26.**G.**
Dar. 10—29/3/26.**L.**

Dar. 14/3—19/5/28.**G.**
Anti-vacuum valves fitted.
Dar. 3/3—29/4/30.**G.**
???. 3—27/3/31.**N/C.**
Dar. 19/6—24/8/31.**H.**
???. 2—12/5/32.**N/C.**
Dar. 7/9—20/10/33.**G.**
???. 22—31/8/34.**N/C.**
Dar. 29/10—30/11/34.
Tender repair.
Dar. 26/2/35.
Tender only.
Dar. 5/3/35.
Tender only.
Dar. 13/3/35.
Tender only.
Dar. 26/8—30/9/35.**G.**
Dar. 6/4/36.*Weigh.*
Tender only.
Dar. 19/8/36.*Weigh.*
Tender only.
Dar. 1/6—10/7/37.**G.**
Dar. 20/12/37—22/12/37.**N/C.**
Dar. 27/6—11/8/38.**H.**
Dar. 8/11/39.*Weigh.*
Dar. 22/4—4/6/40.**G.**
Dar. 13/1—12/2/41.**H.**
Dar. 31/3—9/5/41.**L.**
After collision.
Dar. 30/4—11/6/42.**H/I.**
Dar. 17/9—13/10/42.**N/C.**
Dar. 11/11—16/12/43.**G.**
Dar. 6/11/47. *Not repaired.*

BOILERS:
 G419.
 G358 *(ex649)* ?/12/10.
 G419 *(ex spare)* ?/12/12.
 D851 *(new; sup)* ?/11/19.
 D319 *(exC7 2164)* 10/2/26.
 2288 *(new)* 29/4/30.
D1598 *(exC7 2209)* 20/10/33.
 2147 *(ex704)* 30/9/35.
 2420 *(ex1776)* 10/7/37.
D1497 *(ex742)* 4/6/40.
D1637 *(exC7 729)* 16/12/43.

SHEDS:
Heaton.
York 12/2/25.
Darlington 5/7/34.
Heaton 6/11/40.
Gateshead 28/3/43.

RENUMBERED:
2934 30/6/46.

CONDEMNED: 15/11/47.
Cut up at Darlington.

___

1753

Gateshead 15.

To traffic 8/1904.

REPAIRS:
???. ?/?—?/8/10.**G.**
???. ?/?—?/9/17.**G.**
???. ?/?—11/10/22.**G.**
Ghd. 10/11/23—10/1/24.**L.**
Ghd. 11/3—4/7/24.**G.**
Ghd. 17—30/9/25.**L.**
Ghd. 16/2—13/7/27.**G.**
Anti-vacuum valves fitted.
Ghd. 18—24/2/28.**L.**
Ghd. 17/5—6/7/28.**L.**
Ghd. 17/12/28—15/3/29.**G.**
Ghd. 12—14/6/29.**N/C.**
Ghd. 2/10—11/11/29.
Tender only.
Ghd. 1—14/7/30.**L.**
Ghd. 11/5—1/7/31.**G.**
Ghd. 6/4—14/6/32.**H.**
Dar. 6/2—23/3/34.**G.**
Dar. 24/12/34—8/2/35.**L.**
Dar. 21/6—8/8/36.**G.**
Screw reverse fitted.
Dar. 19/1—4/2/37.**N/C.**
Dar. 24/8—1/10/37.
Tender only.
Dar. 24/5—11/8/38.**L.**
Dar. 24/1—12/5/39.**H.**
Dar. 13/5—13/6/40.**G.**
Dar. 2/2/42.**N/C.**
Dar. 24/9—31/10/42.**G.**
Dar. 17/6/46. *Not repaired.*

BOILERS:
 G421.
 G852 *(new)* ?/8/10.
 G821 *(ex742; sup)* ?/9/17.
 D1637 *(new)* 4/7/24.
 D423 *(exC7 721)* 15/3/29.
 D1662 *(exC7 2197)* 1/7/31.
 2577 *(new)* 23/3/34.
 2420 *(ex1680)* 13/6/40.
 D1656 *(exC7 2165)* 31/10/42.

SHEDS:
Gateshead.
Darlington 4/11/38.
Hull Springhead 28/3/43.
Hull Dairycoates 13/5/44.

RENUMBERED:
Allocated **2935***.*

CONDEMNED: 20/7/46.
Cut up at Darlington.

___

1776

Gateshead 16.

To traffic 10/1904.

REPAIRS:
???. ?/?—?/6/10.**G.**
???. ?/?—?/12/12.**G.**
???. ?/?—?/12/16.**G.**
???. ?/?—23/11/22.**G.**
Ghd. 10—27/7/23.**L.**
Ghd. 3/6—8/7/24.**L.**
Ghd. 27/1—29/4/26.**G.**
Ghd. 24/5—1/6/27.**L.**
Ghd. 9—27/3/28.**L.**
Dar. 21/5—23/6/28.**G.**
Anti-vacuum valves fitted.
Ghd. 5/4—24/7/29.**G.**
Ghd. 4/7—25/8/30.**H.**
Ghd. 11—17/9/30.**N/C.**
Dar. 21/10—11/11/30.**N/C.**
Ghd. 7/10—12/11/31.
Tender only.
Dar. 17/6—18/8/33.
Tender only.
Dar. 2/9—24/10/34.**G.**
Dar. 4/3—28/4/37.**G.**
Screw reverse fitted.
Dar. 6—21/10/38.**L.**
Dar. 10/6/40.*Weigh.*
Dar. 5/9—18/10/40.**G.**
Dar. 20/3/44. *Not repaired.*

BOILERS:
 G422.
 G420 *(ex742)* ?/6/10.
 G371 *(ex295)* ?/12/12.
 D547 *(new; sup)* ?/12/16.
 D397 *(exC7 2193)* 29/4/26.
 D430 *(exC7 721)* 25/8/30.
 2420 *(exC7 2172)* 24/10/34.
 D1412 *(ex532)* 28/4/37.
 2680 *(ex705)* 18/10/40.

SHEDS:
Heaton.
York 4/7/38.
Bridlington 2/6/39.
Heaton 26/11/40.
Hull Springhead 28/3/43.

RENUMBERED:
Allocated **2936***.*

CONDEMNED: 8/4/44.
Cut up at Darlington.

___

By June 1928, when No.1776 was fitted, all twenty had the GE type anti-vacuum valves and except on one boiler, kept them to withdrawal.

The exception was No.705 which in July 1935 was fitted with a newly built boiler which had the normal Gresley type anti-vacuum valve, and which it kept at least until August 1940.

Boilers built from April 1914 had two Ross 'pop' safety valves usually on a mounting and with a cover around their base.

Where the mounting was omitted, but the base cover was still used, then it gave the impression that shorter 'pops' had been fitted.

(above) From the middle 1930's there were odd cases where the base cover was left off, but this was definitely unusual.

Normal whistle gear was a pair of bell shape on a twin mounting, in front of the cab.

In some cases, the larger bell shape - on the driver's side, was replaced by an organ pipe type, but some still had twin bell shape at withdrawal - *see* page 28, bottom.

Until 1933 no sightscreens were provided on the cab side. Note the outlet for the superheater pyrometer tube, although all these guides to steam temperature had gone from the C6's before Grouping. This boiler, new in 1914, was C7 class No.2163's original.

From 6th January 1933 on No.704, all were fitted with triplex glass hinged sightscreen on the cab sides as they went through works, but it took until October 1935 to complete this job with No.702 being the last. Haymarket shed.

The first five built, Nos.532, 649, 784, 295 and 1680, had screw operated reversing gear and retained this type to withdrawal.

The remaining fifteen had steam operated reversing gear and this was the two-handle type which they retained until after April 1928.

The Darlington drawing for the C6 class to have the improved single-handle type of reversing gear, is dated April 1928 but no evidence of change has been found that any were done whilst they still had the number on the tender i.e. until after March 1929. Darlington.

CLASS C 6

1792	**1794**	**696**	**697**

1792

Gateshead 17.

To traffic 10/1904.

REPAIRS:
???. ?/?—?/8/09.**G.**
???. ?/?—?/1/13.**G.**
???. ?/?—?/6/15.**G.**
Dar. 1/3—25/6/23.**G.**
Dar. 12/9—4/10/23.**L.**
Dar. 12/12/23—19/1/24.**L.**
Dar. 19/2—14/3/24.**L.**
Dar. 16/4—29/5/24.**N/C.**
Dar. 24/6—19/9/24.**G.**
Dar. 28/2—19/9/27.**G.**
Anti-vacuum valves fitted.
Dar. 29/4—15/7/29.**G.**
Dar. 29/10—8/11/29.**N/C.**
Dar. 9/6—28/8/31.**G.**
Dar. 30/8—12/9/32.**L.**
Dar. 10/7—5/9/34.**G.**
Dar. 22/8—4/10/35.**H.**
Dar. 22/3—1/7/38.**L.**
Dar. 11/11/38—28/1/39.**G.**
Screw reverse fitted.
Dar. 30/1—16/2/39.**N/C.**
Dar. 13/2—20/3/40.
Tender only.
Dar. 20/5—28/6/41.**L.**
Dar. 26/11—29/12/41.**N/C.**
Dar. 13/7—26/8/42.**G.**
Dar. 28/2/48. *Not repaired.*

BOILERS:
  G423.
  G418 *(ex295)* ?/8/09.
  G423 *(ex1794)* ?/1/13.
  D385 *(new; sup)* ?/6/15.
D1460 *(exC7 2199)* 28/8/31.
D1586 *(ex649)* 5/9/34.
D1473 *(ex702)* 28/1/39.
D1451 *(exC7 737)* 26/8/42.

SHEDS:
York.
Bridlington 12/6/39.
Gateshead 9/12/40.

RENUMBERED:
2937 3/11/46.

CONDEMNED: 13/3/48.
Cut up at Darlington.

1794

Gateshead 18.

To traffic 10/1904.

REPAIRS:
???. ?/?—?/1/10.**G.**
???. ?/?—?/6/12.**G.**
???. ?/?—?/5/16.**G.**
Dar. 26/2—13/5/24.**G.**
Ghd. 12—23/1/25.**L.**
Ghd. 29/9/26—2/2/27.**G.**
Anti-vacuum valves fitted.
Dar. 10/5—21/6/27.**L.**
Ghd. 21/10—9/11/27.**L.**
Ghd. 17—24/11/27.**L.**
Dar. 18/4—26/6/28.**G.**
Dar. 18—19/7/28.**N/C.**
Ghd. 14/1—20/3/29.**G.**
Ghd. 15—30/5/29.**L.**
Ghd. 11—17/10/29.**N/C.**
Ghd. 15/11—4/12/29.**L.**
Ghd. 28/8—12/9/30.**L.**
Ghd. 30/10—15/12/31.**G.**
Dar. 30/5—10/7/33.**L.**
Dar. 29/11/34—8/3/35.**G.**
Dar. 19/4—23/6/37.**G.**
Screw reverse fitted.
Dar. 13/1—8/4/38.
Tender only.
Dar. 2/3—12/4/39.**L.**
Dar. 1/4—17/5/41.**G.**
Dar. 8/5/44. *Not repaired.*

BOILERS:
  G424.
  G423 *(ex1792)* ?/1/10.
  G532 *(ex spare)* ?/6/12.
  D532 *(new; sup)* ?/5/16.
  D315 *(exC7 2164)* 13/5/24.
  D547 *(ex1776)* 2/2/27.
  D851 *(exC7 2163)* 26/6/28.
  D515 *(exC7 2201)* 15/12/31.
  2158 *(exC7 2199)* 8/3/35.
  2461 *(exC7 2163)* 17/5/41.

SHEDS:
Gateshead.
Neville Hill 4/7/38.
Bridlington 31/7/39.
Heaton 9/12/40.
Hull Springhead 28/3/43.
Hull Dairycoates 18/10/43.

RENUMBERED:
Allocated **2938.**

CONDEMNED: 27/5/44.
Cut up at Darlington.

696

Darlington.

To traffic 5/1910.

REPAIRS:
???. ?/?—?/7/13.**G.**
???. ?/?—?/6/15.**G.**
Ghd. 5/10—22/12/23.**G.**
Dar. 28/7—24/9/24.**L.**
Ghd. 25/9—11/12/25.**G.**
Ghd. 4/2—4/5/28.**G.**
Anti-vacuum valves fitted.
Ghd. 17/4—12/6/30.**G.**
Ghd. 17—24/3/32.**N/C.**
Dar. 19/1—18/3/33.**G.**
Dar. 31/10—15/11/33.**N/C.**
Dar. 4/5—4/6/34.
Tender only.
Dar. 14/3—12/7/35.**G.**
Dar. 19/10—10/12/37.
Tender only.
Dar. 6/3—22/4/39.**G.**
Screw reverse fitted.
Dar. 25/9—10/10/39.
Tender only.
Dar. 24/10—1/12/41.**G.**
Dar. 20/10—29/12/44.**G.**

BOILERS:
D2037.
  G420 *(ex1776)* ?/7/13.
  D462 *(new; sup)* ?/6/15.
  D603 *(exC7 2212)* 11/12/25.
  D520 *(exC7 2168)* 4/5/28.
  2305 *(new)* 12/6/30.
D1799 *(ex295)* 12/7/35.
  2144 *(exC7 2204)* 22/4/39.
  2679 *(exC7 2204)* 1/12/41.
  2297 *(exC7 2172)* 29/12/44.

SHEDS:
Gateshead.
Tweedmouth 19/3/27.
Gateshead 9/6/30.
Darlington 5/11/38.
Cudworth 28/3/43.
Hull Dairycoates 8/10/44.

RENUMBERED:
2939 8/12/46.

CONDEMNED: 31/12/47.
Cut up at Darington.

697

Darlington.

To traffic 5/1910.

REPAIRS:
???. ?/?—?/10/13.**G.**
???. ?/?—?/3/20.**G.**
Ghd. ?/?—19/10/22.**G.**
Ghd. 28/3—17/7/25.**G.**
Ghd. 16/6—16/9/27.**G.**
Anti-vacuum valves fitted.
Dar. 28/5—28/6/29.**N/C.**
Dar. 14/4—14/5/30.**G.**
Dar. 20/9—23/2/33.**G.**
Dar. 16/1—6/3/36.**G.**
Screw reverse fitted.
Dar. 4/10/38.*Weigh.*
Dar. 30—31/1/39.**N/C.**
Dar. 27/3—26/5/39.**G.**
Dar. 31/5—13/6/39.**N/C.**
Dar. 1/6/40.*Weigh.*
Dar. 30/4—1/6/42.**G.**
Dar. 22/10/42.*Weigh.*
Dar. 15/9/45. *Not repaired.*

BOILERS:
D2038.
D2037 *(ex696)* ?/10/13.
D2044 *(ex spare;sup)* ?/3/20.
D1957 *(new)* 16/9/27.
D1951 *(exC7 2193)* 23/2/33.
  2428 *(exC7 2211)* 6/3/36.
D1799 *(ex696)* 26/5/39.
  2280 *(exC7 2172)* 1/6/42.

SHEDS:
Tweedmouth.
Darlington 30/4/28.
Cudworth 28/3/43.
Hull Dairycoates 8/10/44.

RENUMBERED:
Allocated **2940.**

CONDEMNED: 13/10/45.
Cut up at Darlington.

698

Darlington.

To traffic 6/1910.

REPAIRS:
???. ?/?—?/7/14.**G.**
???. ?/?—?/8/16.**G.**
???. ?/?—?/3/20.**G.**
???. ?/?—?/3/22.**G.**

WORKS CODES:- Cw - Cowlairs. Dar- Darlington. Don - Doncaster. Ghd - Gateshead. Gor - Gorton. Inv - Inverurie. Nor - Norwich. Str - Stratford.
REPAIR CODES:- **C/H** - Casual Heavy. **C/L** - Casual Light. **G** - General. **H** - Heavy. **H/I** - Heavy Intermediate. **L** - Light. **L/I** - Light Intermediate. **N/C** - Non-Classified.

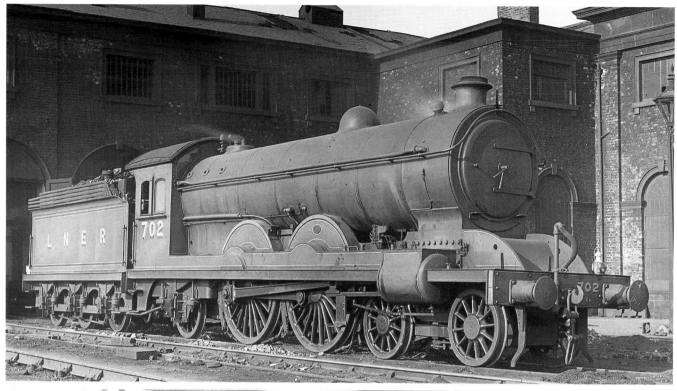

(above) A later modification to the single-handle gear was to move the steam supply control valve from inside the cab to the outlet on the side of the boiler. This was possible because the valve only needed to be closed when the engine was under repair. Darlington.

(left) This 1925 built boiler had only one steam outlet for the steam reverse and apart from this one used on C6 class from September 1932 to October 1934 it served entirely on six different C7 class engines. Note that the right hand anti-vacuum valve has been temporarily blanked off.

Beginning with No.697 in March 1936, all fifteen that had the steam reversing gear changed to screw operated. No.696 in April 1939 completed the process. Low Fell, 25th May 1939 with V2 No.4780.

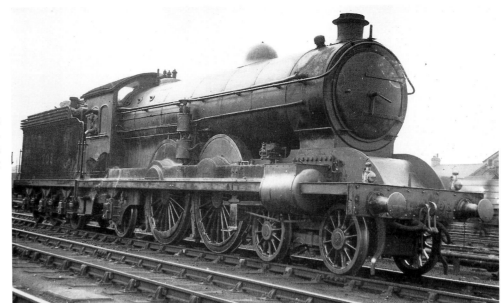

The frames of the first ten did not permit lifting holes to be put in. The deeper, stronger frames at the front of Nos.696 to 705 also did not have lifting holes prior to 1932.

Beginning in early 1932 it became standard to have lifting holes and No.703 got them at a light repair in October of that year.

At superheating an NER designed mechanical lubricator was put on to feed the cylinders and valves. Mounted on the top edge of the frame, it was driven off the inside motion.

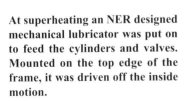

698 cont./
Dar. 18/7—28/9/23.**G.**
Dar. 24/10—10/11/23.**L.**
Speedometer fitted.
Dar. 9/12/24—25/3/25.**L.**
Dar. 23/10/25—16/2/26.**G.**
Dar. 22/2—3/3/26.**L.**
Dar. 5—12/3/26.**L.**
Ghd. 28/7—13/8/26.**L.**
Dar. 25/1—14/4/28.**G.**
Anti-vacuum valves fitted.
Dar. 14/11/29—4/2/30.**G.**
Dar. 20/4—8/6/32.**G.**
Westinghouse to Steam brake.
Dar. 21/6—17/7/34.**L.**
Dar. 26/8—11/10/35.**G.**
Dar. 16/6—17/8/37.**G.**
Screw reverse fitted.
Dar. 14/9/37. *Weigh.*
Dar. 22/4—3/7/39.**N/C.**
Dar. 16/11/39—5/1/40.**G.**
Dar. 1—11/3/40.**N/C.**
Dar. 26/11—27/12/41.**G.**
Dar. 6/12/44—9/2/45.**G.**
Dar. 8/12/47. *Not repaired.*

BOILERS:
D2039.
D2045 *(ex704:sup)* ?/7/14.
D2043 *(ex spare)* ?/8/16.
D2045 *(ex699)* ?/3/20.
NBL19465 *(exC7 721)* ?/3/22.
D1473 *(new)* 28/9/23.
  D310 *(exC7 2206)* 14/4/28.
  2283 *(new)* 4/2/30.
D1598 *(ex1680)* 11/10/35.
  2275 *(ex700)* 17/8/37.
  2056 *(ex703)* 5/1/40.
  2144 *(ex696)* 27/12/41.

SHEDS:
York.
Scarborough 6/7/39.
York 11/3/40.
Hull Dairycoates 28/3/43.
Hull Springhead 8/11/43.
Hull Dairycoates 13/5/44.

RENUMBERED:
2941 15/12/46.

CONDEMNED: 27/12/47.
Cut up at Darlington.

699

Darlington.

To traffic 6/1910.

REPAIRS:
???. ?/?—?/6/14.**G.**
???. ?/?—?/11/17.**G.**
???. ?/?—?/11/19.**G.**

???. ?/?—?/6/21.**G.**
Dar. 1/8—18/10/23.**G.**
Dar. 27/8—22/9/24.**L.**
Dar. 28/4—12/6/25.**L.**
Ghd. 15/10—10/12/26.**G.**
Anti-vacuum valves fitted.
Dar. 16/11/28—8/2/29.**G.**
Ghd. 20/5—21/7/31.**G.**
Ghd. 14—27/8/31.**N/C.**
Dar. 6—14/10/31.**N/C.**
Dar. 14/9—26/10/32.**H.**
Dar. 11/1—2/2/33.
Tender only.
Dar. 19/12/33—1/2/34.**G.**
Dar. 28/8—10/10/34.**H.**
Dar. 1/8/35. *Weigh.*
Dar. 23/3—13/5/36.**G.**
Screw reverse fitted.
Dar. 6/4—7/5/37.**L.**
Dar. 3/8—9/9/37.**H.**
Dar. 20/6—19/8/38.**G.**
Dar. 20/10—19/11/40.
Tender only.
Dar. 20/8—3/9/41.**N/C.**
Dar. 3/2—6/3/42.**G.**
Dar. 13/6/44. *Not repaired.*

BOILERS:
D2040.
D2041 *(ex700;sup)* ?/6/14.
D2045 *(ex spare)* ?/11/17.
D2040 *(ex705)* ?/11/19.
D2039 *(ex702)* ?/6/21.
  D459 *(exC7 2205)* 18/10/23.
D1615 *(exC7 716)* 8/2/29.
  D781 *(ex295)* 26/10/32.
  2060 *(exC7 2200)* 1/2/34.
  2298 *(exC7 2193)* 13/5/36.
  2283 *(exC7 2211)* 19/8/38.
  2165 *(exC7 718)* 6/3/42.

SHEDS:
York.
Tweedmouth 23/2/29.
Gateshead 9/6/30.
Scarborough 30/5/39.
Darlington 3/2/40.
Hull Springhead 28/3/43.
Hull Dairycoates 18/10/43.

RENUMBERED:
Allocated **2942**.

CONDEMNED: 1/7/44.
Cut up at Darlington.

700

Darlington.

To traffic 7/1910.

REPAIRS:
???. ?/?—?/9/14.**G.**

???. ?/?—?/7/18.**G.**
Ghd. 22—29/5/23.**L.**
Dar. 27/2—30/5/24.**G.**
Ghd. 1—5/7/24.**L.**
Ghd. 17/3—.28/6/27**G.**
Anti-vacuum valves fitted.
Ghd. 18—22/5/28.**L.**
Ghd. 15/8—3/9/29.
Tender only.
Ghd. 20/10—21/12/29.**G.**
Ghd. 29/1—6/2/30.**L.**
Ghd. 20/7—9/9/32.**G.**
Westinghouse to Steam brake.
Dar. 23/10—1/12/34.**G.**
Dar. 24/6—17/7/35.**L.**
Dar. 1/4—20/5/37.**G.**
Screw reverse fitted.
Dar. 1/2—6/4/39.**H.**
Dar. 15/7—24/8/40.**G.**
Dar. 26/6—8/7/41.**N/C.**
Dar. 7/4—11/5/43.**G.**
Ghd. 20/2—14/3/45.**L.**
Dar. 10/4/46. *Not repaired..*

BOILERS:
D2041.
D2044 *(ex703)* ?/9/14.
  D767 *(new; sup)* ?/7/18.
D1798 *(exC7 2201)* 9/9/32.
  2275 *(ex701)* 1/12/34.
D1671 *(exC7 2164)* 20/5/37.
D1615 *(ex295)* 24/8/40.
  2418 *(exC7 716)* 11/5/43.

SHEDS:
Tweedmouth.
Gateshead 9/6/30.
Neville Hill 4/7/38.
Bridlington 3/6/39.
Gateshead 9/12/40.

RENUMBERED:
Allocated **2943**.

CONDEMNED: 18/5/46.
Cut up at Darlington.

701

Darlington.

To traffic 7/1910.

REPAIRS:
???. ?/?—?/5/18.**G.**
???. ?/?—?/5/22.**G.**
Dar. 27/2—27/5/24.**G.**
Ghd. 17/6—7/7/25.**L.**
Ghd. 9/10—4/11/25.**L.**
Ghd. 21/12/26—15/6/27.**G.**
Anti-vacuum valves fitted.
Ghd. 29/6—7/7/27.**L.**
Ghd. 21—23/12/27.**L.**
Ghd. 31/3—27/4/28.

Tender only.
Ghd. 3/7—24/8/28.**L.**
Ghd. 17/6—17/9/29.**G.**
Dar. 11/8—25/9/31.**G.**
Dar. 29/8—21/9/33.**L.**
Dar. 12/10—19/11/34.**G.**
Dar. 7—16/8/35.**N/C.**
Dar. 28/4—30/5/36.**L.**
After collision.
Dar. 5/10—25/11/37.**G.**
Screw reverse fitted.
Dar. 11/7—17/8/40.**G.**
Dar. 11/2—5/3/43.**N/C.**
Dar. 9/8/44. *Not repaired.*

BOILERS:
D2042.
  G852 *(ex1753; sup)* ?/5/18.
NBL19451 *(exC7 737)* ?/5/22.
  2275 *(new)* 17/9/29.
  2432 *(exC7 709)* 19/11/34.
  2147 *(ex1680)* 25/11/37.
D1505 *(exC7 733)* 17/8/40.

SHEDS:
Gateshead.
York 1/5/30.
Scarborough 5/6/39.
York 11/3/40.
Hull Dairycoates 28/3/43.

RENUMBERED:
Allocated **2944**.

CONDEMNED: 19/8/44.
Cut up at Darlington.

702

Darlington.

To traffic 8/1910.

REPAIRS:
???. ?/?—?/9/14.**G.**
???. ?/?—?/2/21.**G.**
Dar. 13/2—23/3/23.**G.**
Dar. 27/8—13/12/24.**G.**
Dar. 21/12/26—9/4/27.**G.**
Anti-vacuum valves fitted.
Dar. 11/10—13/12/29.**G.**
Dar. 24/6—31/8/32.**G.**
Westinghouse to Steam brake.
Dar. 17—30/8/34.
Tender only.
Dar. 7/2/35.*Weigh.*
Dar. 26/8—4/10/35.**G.**
Dar. 11/1/37.**N/C.**
Dar. 24—25/2/37.**N/C.**
Dar. 30/7—20/9/38.**G.**
Screw reverse fitted.
Dar. 3/1/40.*Weigh.*
Dar. 12—28/8/40.**N/C.**
Dar. 9/9—18/10/40.**G.**

(above) **The coupled wheel axles were fed from oil boxes on each splasher and there was a sight feed lubricator in the cab to serve the eccentrics.**

(right) **During 1935, five C6's were fitted with solid bronze axles boxes served from a Wakefield Fountain lubricator in the cab. Note the inverted 'U' loops above the axles to avoid air locks in the pipes. The five were Nos.1794 (March), 696 and 705 (July), 704 (August), 702 (October). Darlington.**

All started with a wheel and a handle for smokebox door fastening, but by Grouping the change to two handles had begun - *see* **page 25, centre.**

The wheel was still to be seen in the middle 1930's and No.649 had one to November 1937, the last one recorded on this class.

Until 1929 all carried NER designed drawhook and buffers with the tapered shank and circular flange. Through to withdrawal they all had wooden sandwich type front buffer beams. York.

Although none were changed until after their number was moved to the cab side from March 1929, it became usual for Group Standard drawhook and buffers to be put on - No.649 in March 1931 was definitely so fitted. All but No.705 have been checked with GS buffers. That one still had NER type to August 1940 but could have changed at that general repair which was its last before it was withdrawn on 18th December 1943 to be cut up at Darlington on 15th January 1944. Haymarket.

Until the system was discarded in October 1933, all were fitted with Raven Fog Signalling Apparatus. The striking toggle can be seen just ahead of the trailing coupled wheel. After October 1933 the apparatus was removed. Sheffield.

The engines built in 1910, Nos.696 to 705, were classified V/09 by the North Eastern, the drawings for a modified V having been completed in 1909. Darlington continued to show the NER letter classification on the buffer beam for at least ten years after the LNER took over, No.702 being ex works with it on 31st August 1932.

Until 1932 the class had Westinghouse air brake for engine and train brakes with a vacuum ejector for alternative train braking. Until 1929 the front-end connections were both under the buffer beam, but for vacuum, a swan-neck standpipe was then fitted - *see* above. No carriage heating connection was ever fitted at the front end.

The Unification of Brakes programme of June 1928 included for C6 class to have a steam brake on the engine and vacuum for the train brakes, but no changes took place until June 1932. By the end of September, six were altered. Nos.295 and 698 (June), 705 (July) and 532, 700, and 702 (September). The instruction was then countermanded and no others were altered.

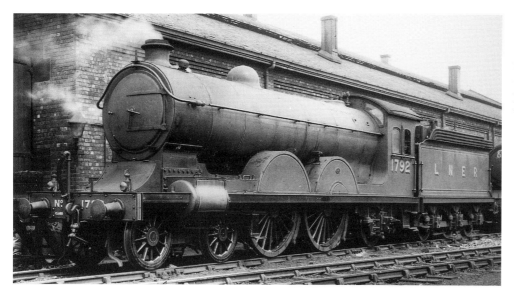

On the remainder, by January 1939 the train pipe connections for the Westinghouse brake were removed and that brake then operated on the engine only. Bridlington, 7th August 1939.

(below) During the late 1930's a minor addition was a drainpipe for the vacuum ejector exhaust. This began inside the smokebox, emerging about on the centre line on the right hand side and dropping down between the frames to dispose of the condensate. Hull Botanic Gardens, August 1939.

(left) On the first ten, sanding was provided in front of the leading coupled and behind the trailing coupled wheels. Until at least 1932 it was air operated from the Westinghouse pump.

(opposite) Some of these ten later had the rear sanding taken off as its need for running in reverse was minimal. When Nos.295 and 532 (see page 21, bottom, also page 20, top) lost the Westinghouse pump in 1932 Their sanding was changed to steam operated, and they did not have rear sanding.

702 cont./
Dar. 27/11/41—28/1/42.**G.**
Dar. 3/9—12/10/43.**G.**
Dar. 17/6/46. *Not repaired..*

BOILERS:
D2043.
D2039 *(ex698;sup)* ?/9/14.
 D330 *(exC7 2168)* ?/2/21.
D1436 *(exC7 2169)* 9/4/27.
D1473 *(exC7 2170)* 31/8/32.
 2298 *(ex699)* 20/9/38.
 2147 *(ex701)* 18/10/40.

SHEDS:
York.
Darlington 2/4/28.
Hull Springhead 28/3/43.
Hull Dairycoates 13/5/44.

RENUMBERED:
Allocated **2945***.*

CONDEMNED: 26/7/46.
Cut up at Darlington.

_____

703

Darlington.

To traffic 8/1910.

REPAIRS:
???. ?/?—?/1/14.**G.**
???. ?/?—?/6/18.**G.**
Ghd. ?/?—3/11/22.**G.**
Ghd. 9—22/10/23.**L.**
Ghd. 16/12/24—30/1/25.**L.**
Ghd. 30/3—10/7/25.**G.**
Ghd. 23/12/26—7/2/27.**L.**
Ghd. 5—8/7/27.**L.**
Ghd. 24/11/27—23/2/28.**G.**
Anti-vacuum valves fitted.
Dar. 3/6—5/9/30.**G.**

Dar. 22/1—2/2/31.**N/C.**
Dar. 20/9—18/10/32.**L.**
Dar. 14/1/33.*Weigh.*
Dar. 12/5/33.
Tender weigh.
Dar. 7/12/33—19/1/34.**G.**
Dar. 20/11/36—12/1/37.**G.**
Screw reverse fitted.
Dar. 18/9—8/11/39.**G.**
Dar. 14/11—4/12/39.**N/C.**
Dar. 26/4—12/5/41.**N/C.**
Dar. 1/7/41.*Weigh.*
Dar. 15/5—24/6/42.**G.**
Dar. 4/1/45. *Not repaired.*

BOILERS:
D2044.
D2038 *(ex697)* ?/1/14.
ₙᵦₗ 19458 *(exC7 734;sup)* 6/18.
 D335 *(exC7 727)* 3/11/22.
 2330 *(new)* 5/9/30.
D1505 *(exC7 2202)* 19/1/34.
 2056 *(ex742)* 12/1/37.
 2841 *(exC7 719)* 8/11/39.
D1799 *(ex697)* 24/6/42.

SHEDS:
Tweedmouth.
Darlington 30/4/28.
Hull Springhead 28/3/43.
Hull Dairycoates 18/10/43.

RENUMBERED:
Allocated **2946***.*

CONDEMNED: 22/1/45.
Cut up at Darlington.

_____

704

Darlington.

To traffic 9/1910.

REPAIRS:
???. ?/?—?/4/14.**G.**
Ghd. 26/3—13/7/23.**G.**
Ghd. 27/10/24—13/1/25.**G.**
Ghd. 11—22/5/25.**L.**
Ghd. 10/1—22/4/27.**G.**
Anti-vacuum valves fitted.
Ghd. 4—18/6/27.**L.**
Ghd. 27/1—14/2/28.**L.**
Ghd. 1/11/28—8/1/29.**G.**
Ghd. 16/9—28/11/29.**L.**
Ghd. 11/6—1/8/30.**G.**
Ghd. 1—5/9/30.**N/C.**
Dar. 10/11/32—6/1/33.**G.**
Owen's regulator valve.
Dar. 17/1/33.**N/C.**
Dar. 2/5—7/8/35.**G.**
Dar. 8—9/8/35.**N/C.**
Dar. 2/12/35.*Weigh.*
Dar. 2/11/36—27/1/37.**L.**
Dar. 15/6—12/8/38.**G.**
Screw reverse fitted.
Dar. 13—22/8/38.**N/C.**
Dar. 15—27/9/38.**N/C.**
Dar. 24/8—30/9/42.**G.**
Dar. 8/11/47. *Not repaired.*

BOILERS:
D2045.
 D310 *(new; sup)* ?/4/14.
 D418 *(exC7 2197)* 13/7/23.
 2165 *(new)* 8/1/29.
 2147 *(exC7 2195)* 6/1/33.
D459 *(ex705)* 7/8/35.
D1456 *(ex784)* 12/8/38.
D1473 *(ex1792)* 30/9/42.

SHEDS:
Gateshead.
Scarborough 31/5/39.
York 11/3/40.
Gateshead 7/12/40.

RENUMBERED:
2947 5/1/47.

CONDEMNED: 22/11/47.
Cut up at Darlington.

_____

705

Darlington.

To traffic 9/1910.

REPAIRS:
???. ?/?—?/8/14.**G.**
???. ?/?—?/7/19.**G.**
???. ?/?—?/2/22.**G.**
Dar. 12/4—10/7/23.**G.**
Ghd. 13/2—14/5/25.**G.**
Ghd. 12—22/1/26.**L.**
Ghd. 18/2—22/7/27.**G.**
Anti-vacuum valves fitted.
Ghd. 21—28/12/27.**L.**
Dar. 10/1—25/3/29.**G.**
Dar. 12/8—3/10/30.**L.**
Dar. 12/5—15/7/32.**G.**
Westinghouse to Steam brake.
Dar. 29/9—18/10/32.**N/C.**
Dar. 17/5—18/7/35.**G.**
Dar. 26/5/36. *Weigh.*
Dar. 9/6/36.
Tender weigh.
Dar. 25/4—1/7/38.**G.**
Screw reverse fitted.
Dar. 19—27/7/38.**N/C.**
Dar. 6/8—20/9/40.**G.**
Dar. 4/8—29/9/41.**L.**
Dar. 27/10—16/11/42.**N/C.**
Dar. 18/11/43. *Not repaired.*

BOILERS:
D2046.
D2040 *(ex699;sup)* ?/8/14.
D2041 *(ex spare)* ?/7/19.
NBL19453 *(exC7 733)* ?/2/22.
D1460 *(new)* 10/7/23.
 D459 *(ex699)* 25/3/29.
 2680 *(new)* 18/7/35.
D1671 *(ex700)* 20/9/40.

SHEDS:
Gateshead.
Darlington 2/4/28.
Hull Springhead 28/3/43.

RENUMBERED:
Allocated **2948***.*

CONDEMNED: 18/12/43.
Cut up at Darlington.

See page 16, top, shows, the 1910 batch had air sanding in front of the leading coupled and to both sides of the trailing coupled wheels. By Grouping only Nos.698 and 702 retained sanding to the front of the trailing wheels, and in the late 1920's No.698 joined the others in having it taken off. On the contrary, No.1792 of the first series, by June 1923 - *see* page 16, top - had gained sanding ahead of the rear-coupled wheels and kept it at least to April 1929 but it was taken off later.

(above) No.702 however, kept the sanding at all three points even after it lost the Westinghouse pump in August 1932 and they were changed to steam operation *see* page 16, top.

This is the odd boiler built in March 1934 to use up surplus Schmidt superheater material and fitted to No.1753 from March 1934 to May 1940 and then to No.295 from July 1940 to March 1944. Note that it had the handholes and not the five washout plugs which were introduced in 1931. Darlington.

The N.E.R. green livery on C6 class included the large armorial on the tender and also the smaller circular version on the rear splasher. No.1776 was ex Gateshead from a general repair on 23rd November 1922 and so retained NER painting until 27th January 1926, being the last C6 to do so. This is a 30th May 1925 photograph at Tweedmouth.

After Grouping, the first to be painted were No.295 (21st March 1923 ex Gateshead) and 702 (23rd March 1923 ex Darlington). As both were still given full NER livery, no C6 thus received L.&N.E.R. One from each works then got L&NER, No.1792 ex Darlington on 25th June 1923 and 704 ex Gateshead 13th July 1923 and then the ampersand was discarded. York.

No.705, ex Darlington on 10th July 1923 was the first C6 to have LNER which became the standard style.

From September 1923 to early in February 1924, the area suffix D was added to the number but it was only applied to three C6, all in 1923; No.698 (28th September) and 699 (18th October) got it at Darlington and No.696 (22nd December) at Gateshead.

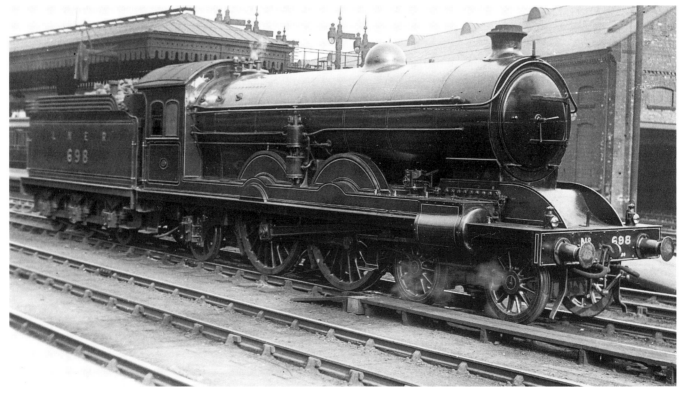

Until Gateshead works closed in January 1933, it was possible to tell at which works a C6 had been painted. Gateshead always left the ends of the sandwich buffer beam in plain black matching the angle of the running plate. On engines painted by Darlington the ends of the buffer beam were panelled with a white line matching that put on the front buffer plate. York.

From March 1929 the number was moved from the tender to the cab. No.1794 on 20th March 1929 was the first from Gateshead and No.1792 on 15th July 1929 the first from Darlington. On the buffer beam Class V and V/09 continued in use until 1932.

It was almost ten years after the LNER classification schedule was adopted before it began to be displayed on ex North Eastern engines and both batches took C6 without any part division. Darlington.

Until November 1941 green livery continued and No.784 had it when ex works 9th August 1941. Six others Nos.532, 649, 701, 705, 1776 and 1794 were still green when they were withdrawn. Gateshead, 25th July 1946.

No.784 was renumbered 2931 on Sunday 24th November 1946 at Gateshead shed by a painter from the works there, which had been reopened during the war. Yellow unshaded figures in Gill sans style but with the modified 9 were put on.

No.742 changed to 2933 during a general repair at Darlington from which it was ex works on 5th October 1946. At that date the tender would have LNER restored to it. The change from green to unlined black was made on 9th March 1943. Scarborough.

No.1680 became 2934 on Sunday 30th June 1946 at Gateshead shed and the use of normal shaded transfers indicates works attention to the job. Change from green to black without lining was effective from 11th June 1942 and to only NE on the tender from 16th December 1943. Gateshead, 1947.

No.1792 was renumbered 2937 on Sunday 3rd November 1946 at Gateshead shed in yellow Gill sans but with a modified 9. It was last ex works on 26th August 1942 and subsequently kept the same tender so in 1942 it must just have squeezed in to get LNER and not just NE on the tender for the duration of the war.

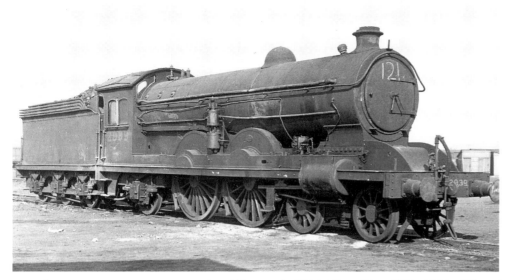

No.696 became 2939 on Sunday 8th December 1946 at Dairycoates shed, the local painter trying to match the displaced black numbers but without shading to them. Tender lettering remained as NE. Dairycoates, 1947.

After No.696 had been renumbered 2939, this engine was used during the latter part of 1947 as a stationary boiler at the water softening plant adjacent to Hessle station but it was withdrawn on 31st December 1947 and cut up at Darlington by 14th January 1948.

No.698 changed to 2941 on Sunday 15th December 1946, unshaded black numbers being put on by a local Hull painter. The tender was only lettered NE, so that no C6 apart from 2933 got the LNER restored. Dairycoates, 17th April 1947.

No.704 was the last C6 to be renumbered, on Sunday 5th January 1947 at Gateshead shed, and a works painter used Gill sans style for 2947 but with the modified 9. Gateshead, 26th April 1947.

Dynamometer car trials soon established the value of superheating and that the first ten should be converted as soon as that could be done conveniently. This took place between May 1914 and April 1915.

The second ten of the order placed with N.B. Loco. Co. and built between August and December 1911, Nos.722, 727, 728, 729, 732, 733, 734, 735, 736 and 737, were fitted with the Schmidt type superheater. For element protection they had a small horizontal steam cylinder on the side of the smokebox. The rod from the cab operated a piston connected to a damper controlling the flow of hot gases through the flues. Note Z1 classification of the early superheated engines. It became just Z in June 1914 when conversion of the first ten had begun.

CLASS C 7

706

N.B. Loco 19446.

To traffic 7/1911.

REPAIRS:
???. ?/?—?/10/14.**G.**
Superheater put in.
???. ?/?—?/8/16.**G.**
Dar. 23/2—30/5/23.**G.**
Ghd. 25/11—18/2/25.**G.**
Dar. 9/2—28/7/27.**G.**
Dar. 13/3—29/5/29.**G.**
Dar. 3/12/30—30/1/31.**G.**
Ghd. 18—23/3/32.**N/C.**
Dar. 18/8—18/10/32.**G.**
Westinghouse to Steam brake.
Dar. 31/5—2/6/33.**N/C.**
Dar. 4/8/33.*Weigh.*
Dar. 12/2—12/4/35.**G.**
*Srew reverse & B16 type springs
fitted.*
Dar. 15/4—13/5/35.**N/C.**
Dar. 31/8—13/11/36.**H.**
Dar. 25/1—4/3/38.**G.**
Dar. 5—23/3/38.**N/C.**
Dar. 9/10—13/11/40.**G.**
Dar. 9/3—3/4/43.**L.**
Dar. 1/4—3/5/44.**G.**
Dar. 14/8/46. *Not repaired.*

BOILERS:
NBL 19446.
NBL 19446 *(sup)* ?/10/14.
NBL 19456 *(ex722)* ?/8/16.
 D426 *(ex2195)* 30/5/23.
 D312 *(ex734)* 18/2/25.
 D330 *(exC6 702)* 28/7/27.
 D508 *(ex2208)* 29/5/29.
 D1656 *(ex728)* 30/1/31.
 D1436 *(exC6 702)* 18/10/32.
 2432 *(exC6 701)* 4/3/38.
 2460 *(ex720)* 13/11/40.
 2680 *(exC6 1776)* 3/5/44.

SHEDS:
Gateshead.
York 21/2/25.
Scarborough 12/3/45.

RENUMBERED:
Allocated **2950**.

CONDEMNED: 21/12/46.
Cut up at Darlington.

709

N.B. Loco 19447.

To traffic 7/1911.

REPAIRS:
???. ?/?—?/10/14.**G.**
???. ?/?—15/6/22.**G.**
Ghd. 13/10/23—17/1/24.**G.**
Ghd. 10/4—24/7/24.**L.**
Ghd. 1/4—22/7/25.**G.**
Ghd. 12—27/4/26.**L.**
Ghd. 16/9—20/1/27.**G.**
Ghd. 12/11—7/12/27.**L.**
Dar. 27/4—25/6/28.**G.**
Dar. 4—13/7/28.**N/C.**
Ghd. 21—29/9/28.**L.**
Ghd. 24/10—8/11/28.**L.**
Ghd. 14/2—7/4/30.**G.**
Dar. 6—30/6/30.**N/C.**
Ghd. 18—21/1/32.**N/C.**
Ghd. 26/4—10/6/32.**G.**
Westinghouse to Steam brake.
Dar. 18/4—9/5/33.**N/C.**
Dar. 21/9—1/11/34.**G.**
Screw reverse fitted.
Dar. 17/2—2/4/37.**G.**
Dar. 29/10—8/11/38.**N/C.**
Dar. 7/5—7/6/40.**G.**
Dar. 13—25/6/40.**N/C.**
Dar. 5—29/6/42.**L.**
Dar. 21/4—24/5/43.**G.**
Dar. 7/3/46. *Not repaired.*

BOILERS:
NBL 19447.
 D371 *(new; sup)* ?/10/14.
 D409 *(ex2196)* 17/1/24.
 D449 *(ex2172)* 25/6/28.
 2432 *(new)* 10/6/32.
 D1460 *(exC6 1792)* 1/11/34.
 2834 *(new)* 2/4/37.
 2687 *(ex2210)* 24/5/43.

SHEDS:
Gateshead.
Neville Hill 22/4/38.
Hull Dairycoates 28/3/43.

RENUMBERED:
Allocated **2951**.

CONDEMNED: 23/3/46.
Cut up at Darlington.

710

N.B. Loco 19448.

To traffic 7/1911.

REPAIRS:
???. ?/?—?/6/14.**G.**
???. ?/?—?/2/18.**G.**
???. ?/?—?/10/22.**G.**
Ghd. 10/4—25/7/24.**G.**
Ghd. 27/7/26—17/1/27.**G.**
Ghd. 13—28/10/27.**L.**
Ghd. 28/4—24/7/28.**G.**
Ghd. 30/5—18/9/29.**H.**
Ghd. 6—28/11/29.
Tender only.
Ghd. 21/3—9/5/30.**G.**
Dar. 5—17/9/30.**N/C.**
Ghd. 30/10—20/11/30.**L.**
Ghd. 22—31/7/31.**L.**
Ghd. 6/10—30/12/31.**H.**
Ghd. 7/3/32.
Tender only.
Dar. 14/11/32—1/2/33.**G.**
Westinghouse to Steam brake.
Dar. 31/10/34—23/1/35.**G.**
Screw reverse fitted.
Dar. 31/10/35—10/2/36.**G.**
Dar. 28/2—28/4/38.**G.**
Dar. 18/12/40—24/1/41.**G.**
Dar. 7/2/44. *Not repaired.*

BOILERS:
NBL 19448.
NBL 19450 *(ex716; sup)* ?/6/14.
NBL 19457 *(ex722)* ?/2/18.
D1430 *(new)* ?/10/22.
 2165 *(exC6 704)* 1/2/33.
 2419 *(ex717)* 23/1/35.
D1953 *(ex2209)* 28/4/38.
 2432 *(ex706)* 24/1/41.

SHEDS:
Heaton.
Neville Hill 5/6/39.
Hull Dairycoates 28/3/43.

RENUMBERED:
Allocated **2952**.

CONDEMNED: 19/2/44.
Cut up at Darlington.

714

N.B. Loco 19449.

To traffic 7/1911.

REPAIRS:
???. ?/?—?/6/14.**G.**
Superheater put in.
???. ?/?—?/2/19.**G.**
???. ?/?—23/3/22.**G.**
Dar. 1/3—31/5/23.**G.**
Ghd. 6/12/24—2/3/25.**G.**
Ghd. 1/7—28/10/27.**G.**
Ghd. 22/4—25/7/29.**G.**
Dar. 8/4—29/5/31.**G.**
Dar. 29/3—5/5/34.**G.**
*Westinghouse to Steam brake, &
screw reverse fitted.*
Dar. 8—21/6/34.**L.**
Dar. 29/2—9/4/36.**G.**
Dar. 13/7—12/8/36.**L.**
Dar. 16/9—9/11/39.**G.**
Dar. 23/7—9/9/41.**G.**
Dar. 15/12/43. *Not repaired.*

BOILERS:
NBL 19449.
NBL 19449 *(sup)* ?/6/14.
 D792 *(new)* ?/2/19.
 D508 *(ex706)* 29/5/31.
 2583 *(new)* 5/5/34.
 2462 *(ex734)* 9/11/39.
D1436 *(ex729)* 9/9/41.

SHEDS:
Haymarket.
St Margarets 16/3/39.
York 2/6/43.

RENUMBERED:
Allocated **2953**.

CONDEMNED: 8/1/44.
Cut up at Darlington.

716

N.B. Loco 19450.

To traffic 7/1911.

REPAIRS:
???. ?/?—?/5/14.**G.**
???. ?/?—?/7/19.**G.**
Ghd. 27/10/22—23/2/23.**G.**

WORKS CODES:- Cw - Cowlairs. Dar- Darlington. Don - Doncaster. Ghd - Gateshead. Gor - Gorton. Inv - Inverurie. Nor - Norwich. Str - Stratford.
REPAIR CODES:- **C/H** - Casual Heavy. **C/L** - Casual Light. **G** - General. **H**- Heavy. **H/I** - Heavy Intermediate. **L** - Light. **L/I** - Light Intermediate. **N/C** - Non-Classified.

The cylinder and damper arrangement was discarded during the 1914-1918 war and the rod from the cab operated a small valve which allowed some steam to pass through the elements. Note that the pyrometer connection has also been taken off.

(above) From May to August 1914, Nos.2163 to 2172 were built by Darlington, all fitted with Schmidt superheater and instead of the control rod from the cab, there was a steam valve with a handwheel fitted on the side of the smokebox. This batch also introduced Ross 'pop' safety valves as the standard fitting henceforward.

(left) A final batch of nineteen, Nos.2193 to 2211, took Darlington works from December 1914 to June 1917 to complete, they differed from Nos.2163-2172 only in having a more modern self-trimming tender.

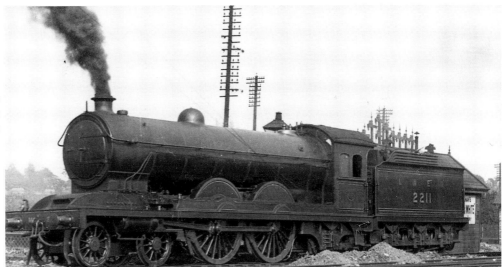

Until 1931, the boilers were provided with two handholes on the left-hand side of the firebox for washout purposes. York.

(above) On the right hand side, three handholes were included, and not directly opposite those on the other side.

(right) The boilers built from November 1931 had Robinson instead of Schmidt superheater. They also had five washout plugs instead of handholes.

716 cont./
Ghd. 10—29/5/23.**L.**
Ghd. 12—20/6/23.**L.**
Ghd. 15/5—6/8/24.**G.**
Ghd. 14/10/26—26/1/27.**G.**
Dar. 7/11/28—9/1/29.**G.**
Ghd. 4/6—30/7/30.**G.**
Dar. 18—29/8/30.**N/C.**
Dar. 28/10—9/12/32.**G.**
Westinghouse to Steam brake.
Dar. 4/3—1/5/35.**H.**
Dar. 15/6—3/9/36.**G.**
Screw reverse fitted.
Dar. 19/12/39—30/1/40.**G.**
Dar. 7/1—5/4/43.**G.**
Dar. 8—28/3/45.**L.**
Dar. 24/12/45—9/2/46.**G.**
Dar. 15/6/48. *Not repaired.*

BOILERS:
NBL 19450.
 D312 *(new; sup)* ?/5/14.
D2042 *(ex spare)* ?/7/19.
D1615 *(new)* 6/8/24.
 D323 *(ex2167)* 9/1/29.
 2298 *(new)* 30/7/30.
D1957 *(exC6 697)* 9/12/32.
 2418 *(ex2208)* 30/1/40.
 2275 *(exC6 742)* 5/4/43.
D1957 *(ex2198)* 9/2/46.

SHEDS:
Gateshead.
York 9/10/24.
Gateshead 9/2/34.
Heaton 28/3/43.
Scarborough 9/3/47.

RENUMBERED:
2954 1/12/46.

CONDEMNED: 26/6/48.
Cut up at Darlington.

717

N.B. Loco 19451.

To traffic 8/1911.

REPAIRS:
???. ?/?—?/4/15.**G.**
???. ?/?—?/10/22.**G.**
Ghd. 9—15/2/23.**L.**
Dar. 9/5—7/8/24.**G.**
Ghd. 12/5—13/8/28.**G.**
Dar. 10/2—12/4/30.**G.**
Dar. 31/10/30—20/1/31.**L.**
Proportional valve fitted.
Dar. 23—24/3/31.**N/C.**
Defective Westinghouse pump replaced.
Dar. 23/10—18/12/31.**N/C.**

Dar. 23/6—8/8/32.**G.**
Westinghouse to Steam brake, & rail washing gear fitted.
Dar. 27/2—6/3/33.**N/C.**
Dar. 2—19/10/33.**N/C.**
Dar. 5/11/34—21/1/35.**G.**
Screw reverse fitted.
Dar. 30/3—30/4/35.**L.**
Dar. 7/8—22/9/36.**G.**
Dar. 25/8—28/10/38.**G.**
Dar. 13/8—27/9/41.**G.**
Dar. 6/10—12/11/43.**L.**
Dar. 15/4/44. *Not repaired.*

BOILERS:
NBL 19451.
NBL 19460 *(ex732; sup)* ?/4/15.
D1635 *(new)* 7/8/24.
 D446 *(ex2204)* 12/4/30.
 2419 *(new)* 8/8/32.
D1497 *(ex737)* 21/1/35.
D1613 *(ex2172)* 22/9/36.
 2421 *(ex2207)* 27/9/41.
 2330 *(ex2202)* 12/11/43.

SHEDS:
Gateshead.
York 15-28/2/23.

RENUMBERED:
Allocated **2955**.

CONDEMNED: 29/4/44.
Cut up at Darlington.

718

N.B. Loco 19452.

To traffic 8/1911.

REPAIRS:
???. ?/?—?/7/14.**G.**
???. ?/?—?/8/19.**G.**
Ghd. 26/10/22—15/2/23.**G.**
Ghd. 15/4—25/7/24.**G.**
Dar. 9/11/26—11/3/27.**G.**
Ghd. 16/11/28—24/1/29.**G.**
Ghd. 16/10—26/11/30.**G.**
Ghd. 24/3—1/4/31.**N/C.**
Dar. 28/11/32—18/1/33.**G.**
Westinghouse to Steam brake.
Dar. 6/12/35—21/3/36.**G.**
Screw reverse fitted.
Dar. 17/1—25/2/39.**G.**
Dar. 27/2—8/3/39.**N/C.**
Dar. 16/9—25/10/41.**G.**
Dar. 12/5—21/6/44.**G.**
Dar. 23/12/44—23/1/45.**L.**
Dar. 27/5/46. *Not repaired.*

BOILERS:
NBL 19452.

NBL 19448 *(ex710; sup)* ?/7/14.
NBL 19459 *(ex727)* ?/8/19.
NBL 19452 *(ex737)* 15/2/23.
 2158 *(new)* 24/1/29.
D1635 *(ex728)* 18/1/33.
 2165 *(ex2164)* 25/2/39.
 2462 *(ex714)* 25/10/41.
D1635 *(ex2200)* 21/6/44.

SHEDS:
Gateshead.
Neville Hill 13/11/24.
Tweedmouth 1/3/28.
Gateshead 22/3/39.
Hull Dairycoates 28/3/43.

RENUMBERED:
2956 23/3/46.

CONDEMNED: 15/6/46.
Cut up at Darlington.

719

N.B. Loco 19453.

To traffic 8/1911.

REPAIRS:
???. ?/?—?/1/15.**G.**
???. ?/?—?/10/20.**G.**
???. ?/?—2/6/22.**G.**
Ghd. 9/7—28/9/23.**G.**
Ghd. 2—16/6/24.**L.**
Ghd. 29/7—2/8/24.**L.**
Ghd. 27/2—8/6/25.**G.**
Ghd. 7/12/26—5/4/27.**G.**
Ghd. 16/5—2/8/28.**G.**
Dar. 19—30/10/28.**N/C.**
Ghd. 11—13/3/29.**N/C.**
Ghd. 27—28/8/29.**N/C.**
Ghd. 9—18/10/29.**N/C.**
Ghd. 5/3—24/4/30.**G.**
Ghd. 19/10—1/12/31.**G.**
Dar. 1—25/4/32.**N/C.**
Dar. 30/4—12/7/35.**G.**
Westinghouse to Steam brake, & screw reverse fitted.
Dar. 20/10/36—8/1/37.**G.**
Dar. 11/1—5/2/37.**N/C.**
Dar. 21/1—14/2/39.**N/C.**
Dar. 20/4—3/6/39.**G.**
Dar. 5—13/6/39.**N/C.**
Dar. 25/2—8/4/41.**G.**
Dar. 15/4/44. *Not repaired.*

BOILERS:
NBL 19453.
NBL 19447 *(ex709; sup)* ?/1/15.
NBL 19446 *(ex735)* ?/10/20.
D1799 *(new)* 5/4/27.
 D463 *(ex734)* 2/8/28.
 2297 *(new)* 24/4/30.

2841 *(new)* 8/1/37.
 2428 *(exC6 697)* 3/6/39.
D1460 *(exC6 532)* 8/4/41.

SHEDS:
Gateshead.
York 3/12/31.

RENUMBERED:
Allocated **2957**.

CONDEMNED: 29/4/44.
Cut up at Darlington.

720

N.B. Loco 19454.

To traffic 8/1911.

REPAIRS:
???. ?/?—?/9/14.**G.**
???. ?/?—?/4/19.**G.**
???. ?/?—?/5/21.**G.**
???. ?/?—25/4/22.**G.**
Ghd. 15/5—20/8/23.**G.**
Ghd. 29/5—7/6/24.**L.**
Ghd. 14/2—8/7/25.**G.**
Ghd. 10—23/12/25.**L.**
Ghd. 22—31/3/26.**L.**
Ghd. 30/11—9/12/26.**L.**
Ghd. 14—23/12/26.**L.**
Ghd. 18/1—13/5/27.**G.**
Ghd. 19—28/1/28.**L.**
Ghd. 4/2—29/4/29.**G.**
Ghd. 12—29/5/30.**L.**
Ghd. 21/5—15/7/31.**G.**
Dar. 24/7—4/9/33.**G.**
Westinghouse to Steam brake.
Dar. 1/7—31/8/36.**G.**
Screw reverse fitted.
Dar. 31/10/39.*Weigh.*
Dar. 10/9—7/11/40.**G.**
Dar. 28/11—17/12/42.**N/C.**
Dar. 19/4—27/5/44.**G.**
Dar. 4—28/8/44.**L.**
Dar. 8/2—19/3/45.**L.**
Dar. 8/10/47. *Not repaired.*

BOILERS:
NBL 19454.
NBL 19452 *(ex718; sup)* ?/9/14.
NBL 19450 *(ex spare)* ?/4/19.
NBL 19455 *(ex spare)* ?/5/21.
D1424 *(ex737)* 13/5/27.
 D312 *(ex2207)* 29/4/29.
 2460 *(new)* 4/9/33.
D1412 *(exC6 1776)* 7/11/40.
 2460 *(ex706)* 27/5/44.

SHEDS:
Gateshead.
Tweedmouth 2/3/28.

(above) **There were five washout plugs also on the left-hand side on a slightly staggered pitching from those opposite.**

(right) **There was one odd boiler built in March 1934 to use up surplus Schmidt superheater material, and this reverted to handholes. After serving on two C6 class, in June 1944 it was put on 2164 (which became 2970 in September 1946) and was scrapped from that engine in November 1947.**

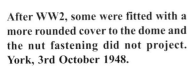

After WW2, some were fitted with a more rounded cover to the dome and the nut fastening did not project. York, 3rd October 1948.

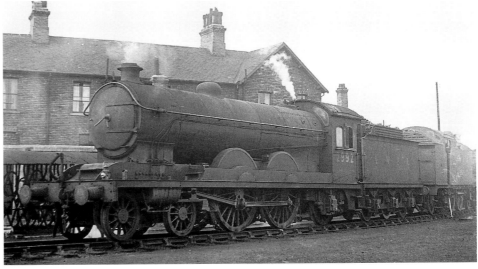

By Grouping, the control from the cab for element protection had largely disappeared and it was very rare to see it with LNER livery. It was more usual for there to be the handwheel valve on the smokebox side for protection of superheater element as on No.2210.

(above) From Gateshead on 27th September 1923, No.2196 was ex works fitted with a Gresley anti-vacuum valve, and anti-carbonisers at the base of the smokebox at the left-hand side. No.735, ex works on 11th March 1924, was the next so treated and henceforth the whole class had this change.

(left) Throughout the whole life of the class, a capuchon on the chimney was carried by the Part 1 engines, only Nos.732 and 2212, after rebuilding to Part 2, being without it. There were odd cases when corrosion caused removal of what remained, but the capuchon was restored at the next works visit.

720 cont./
York 2/6/39.
Scarborough 12/3/45.
Hull Dairycoates 29/9/46.

RENUMBERED:
2958 31/3/46.

CONDEMNED: 8/11/47.
Cut up at Darlington.

721

N.B. Loco 19455.

To traffic 9/1911.

REPAIRS:
???. ?/?—?/6/14.**G**.
Superheater put in.
???. ?/?—?/8/17.**G**.
???. ?/?—?/9/21.**G**.
Ghd. 27/9—15/2/23.**G**.
Dar. 19/3—14/6/24.**G**.
Dar. 1/12/26—17/3/27.**G**.
Dar. 13/12/27—19/1/28.**L**.
Ghd. 26/10—20/12/28.**G**.
Ghd. 12/5—17/7/30.**G**.
Ghd. 30/9—8/10/30.**N/C**.
Ghd. 4—22/11/32.**H**.
Dar. 7/3—3/5/33.**G**.
Westinghouse to Steam brake, &
screw reverse fitted.
Dar. 8—23/5/33.**N/C**.
Dar. 30/4—5/5/34.**N/C**.
Dar. 19/2—5/6/35.**G**.
Dar. 6—17/6/35.**N/C**.
Dar. 14/11—16/12/38.**G**.
Dar. 8/4—19/6/40.**L**.
Dar. 2—14/5/41.**N/C**.
Dar. 13/3—18/4/42.**G**.
Dar. 15/2/44. *Not repaired.*

BOILERS:
NBL 19455.
NBL 19455 *(sup)* ?/6/14.
NBL 19465 *(ex735)* ?/8/17.
NBL 19450 *(ex720)* ?/9/21.
D1451 *(new)* 15/2/23.
  D423 *(ex2202)* 17/3/27.
  D430 *(ex2201)* 20/12/28.
  D532 *(ex2211)* 17/7/30.
D1615 *(exC6 699)* 22/11/32.
  2280 *(ex2166)* 5/6/35.
  2057 *(ex737)* 16/12/38.
  2835 *(ex728)* 18/4/42.

SHEDS:
Gateshead.
York ?/2/23.
Gateshead 2/6/28.
Darlington 28/3/43.

RENUMBERED:
Allocated **2959**.

CONDEMNED: 26/2/44.
Cut up at Darlington.

722

N.B. Loco 19456.

To traffic 8/1911.

REPAIRS:
???. ?/?—?/1/16.**G**.
???. ?/?—?/12/17.**G**.
???. ?/?—?/9/21.**G**.
Dar. 5/1—30/4/23.**G**.
Ghd. 20/5—13/8/24.**G**.
Ghd. 25/1—17/5/26.**G**.
Ghd. 6—16/5/27.**L**.
Ghd. 7/11/27—28/2/28.**G**.
Ghd. 13—14/11/28.**N/C**.
Ghd. 25/9—6/12/29.**G**.
Ghd. 30/11/31—1/2/32.**G**.
Ghd. 17—22/8/32.**L**.
Dar. 21/11/34—12/7/35.**G**.
Westinghouse to Steam brake, &
screw reverse fitted.
Dar. 6/1—11/2/36.**L**.
Dar. 12—23/10/36.**N/C**.
Dar. 20/9—29/10/38.**G**.
Dar. 25/2—9/4/41.**G**.
Dar. 18/11/43—15/1/44.**G**.
Dar. 15—23/2/46.**L**.
Dar. 2—27/3/46.**L**.
Dar. 25/1/47. *Not repaired.*

BOILERS:
NBL 19456.
NBL 19457 *(ex727)* ?/1/16.
NBL 19463 *(ex727)* ?/12/17.
NBL 19461 *(ex spare)* ?/9/21.
  2056 *(new)* 28/2/28.
  D851 *(exC6 1794)* 1/2/32.
  2679 *(new)* 12/7/35.
  2424 *(ex2207)* 29/10/38.
D1953 *(ex710)* 9/4/41.
D1497 *(exC6 1680)* 15/1/44.

SHEDS:
Gateshead.
Neville Hill 22/4/38.
Hull Dairycoates 28/3/43.
York 26/11/45.
Scarborough 30/12/46.

RENUMBERED:
2960 26/3/46.

CONDEMNED: 8/3/47.
Cut up at Darlington.

727

N.B. Loco 19457.

To traffic 9/1911.

REPAIRS:
???. ?/?—?/9/15.**G**.
???. ?/?—?/7/17.**G**.
???. ?/?—?/7/19.**G**.
???. ?/?—?/4/21.**G**.
???. ?/?—?/9/22.**G**.
Ghd. 19/4—5/7/23.**G**.
Dar. 14/6—13/9/24.**G**.
Dar. 13/1—13/6/27.**G**.
Dar. 9—24/3/28.**L**.
Dar. 31/1—12/4/29.**G**.
Dar. 23/1/31.
Rebuilt to Class C9.

BOILERS:
NBL 19457.
NBL 19463 *(ex735)* ?/9/15.
NBL 19459 *(ex spare)* ?/7/17.
NBL 19452 *(ex720)* ?/7/19.
  D335 *(ex2170)* ?/4/21.
NBL 19462 *(ex735)* ?/9/22.
D1451 *(ex721)* 13/6/27.

SHEDS:
Gateshead.
York 21/2/25.

728

N.B. Loco 19458.

To traffic 9/1911.

REPAIRS:
???. ?/?—?/8/15.**G**.
???. ?/?—?/5/20.**G**.
Ghd. 7/1—8/4/24.**G**.
Gresley snifter and
anti-carbonisers fitted.
Ghd. 29/7—7/8/24.**L**.
Ghd. 12/11/25—22/2/26.**G**.
Ghd. 16—18/8/27.**L**.
Dar. 10/10/27—15/2/28.**G**.
A.C.F.I. fitted.
Dar. 18—24/4/28.**N/C**.
Dar. 31/7—8/8/28.**N/C**.
Dar. 14/3—4/4/29.**N/C**.
Dar. 29/4—11/8/30.**G**.
Dar. 22/8—26/9/30.**N/C**.
Dar. 15/1—16/2/31.**H**.
Dar. 6—19/10/31.**N/C**.
Dar. 15/1—22/2/32.**H**.
Dar. 11/11—6/12/32.**G**.
Westinghouse to Steam brake.
Dar. 17/10/33—1/12/33.**L**.
Dar. 6/8—23/9/35.**G**.
Screw reverse fitted.

Dar. 15—25/8/36.**N/C**.
Dar. 21/1—2/3/37.**N/C**.
Dar. 6/9—26/10/38.**G**.
Dar. 2/3—4/4/42.**G**.
A.C.F.I. removed.
Dar. 15—27/6/42.**N/C**.
Dar. 10/10/45. *Not repaired.*

BOILERS:
NBL 19458.
NBL 19461 *(ex733)* ?/8/15.
D2038 *(ex spare)* ?/5/20.
D1656 *(new)* 22/2/26.
D1635 *(ex717)* 11/8/30.
D1656 *(ex706)* 6/12/32.
  2693 *(new)* 23/9/35.
  2835 *(new)* 26/10/38.
  2427 *(ex2193)* 4/4/42.

SHEDS:
Gateshead.
York 10/5/29.
Scarborough 12/3/45.

RENUMBERED:
Allocated **2961**.

CONDEMNED: 17/11/45.
Cut up at Darlington.

729

N.B. Loco 19459.

To traffic 9/1911.

REPAIRS:
???. ?/?—?/5/16.**G**.
Dar. 4/3—14/6/24.**G**.
Ghd. 18/5—17/9/26.**H**.
Dar. 4/4—19/6/28.**G**.
Ghd. 26/3—15/5/30.**G**.
Ghd. 27/1—10/3/32.**G**.
Westinghouse to Steam brake.
Dar. 5/11/34—10/1/35.**G**.
Screw reverse fitted.
Dar. 2/3—6/5/38.**G**.
Dar. 6—18/5/38.**N/C**.
Dar. 6/3—19/4/41.**G**.
Dar. 29/9—30/10/43.**G**.
Dar. 27/1—21/2/44.**L**.
Ghd. 21/1—17/2/45.**L**.
Dar. 20/10/45. *Not repaired.*

BOILERS:
NBL 19459.
NBL 19464 *(ex736)* ?/5/16.
D1671 *(new)* 17/9/26.
  2421 *(new)* 10/3/32.
D1436 *(ex706)* 6/5/38.
D1637 *(ex2196)* 19/4/41.
  2428 *(ex2163)* 30/10/43.

The normal depth of capuchon was 2¹⁄₂in. but for some reason Gateshead turned out No.2207 on 20th March 1929 with one 4in. deep. No others were so noted and 2207 soon reverted to normal.

The 1911 contractor built engines had Ramsbottom safety valves enclosed by a large polished brass cover. Only one of this type - boiler D2039 survived to run in LNER paint. It was used by No.2197 from 30th May 1924 to 8th December 1925 and then changed to 'pop' safety valves. Boiler D2039 was first put on C6 class No.698 when new in June 1910. Tweedmouth.

When Ross 'pops' were put on a Ramsbottom mounting they gave the impression of being a taller variety. This was boiler No.19462 which originally had Ramsbottom safety valves.

This was a replacement boiler for C6 class built in 1918 on which the 'pops' were fitted directly on to the firebox. This lower mounting position made them appear to be shorter.

Only rarely were this class in traffic without the base cover to the safety valves, most survived to withdrawal.

(above) **No.2981 at Darlington shed on 16th August 1947 with a 1932 built boiler and safety valve base cover still in place. It was last ex works on 29th June 1944 and was not repaired again before it was withdrawn on 9th July 1948.**

(left) **On all the first twenty, the whistles were one large and one small bell shape on a twin mounting in front of the cab.**

(below) **On most of the first twenty the larger bell shape was later changed to the organ pipe type. Grantham.**

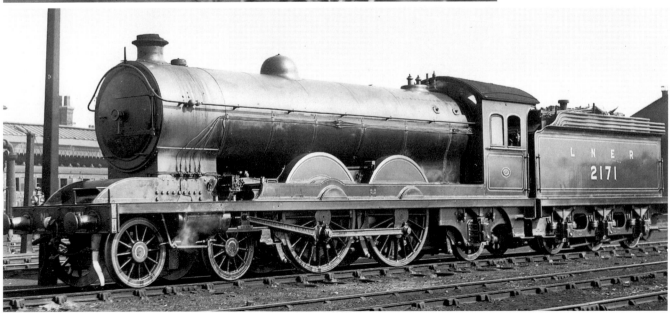

(above) **After having changed to the organ pipe type -** *see* **page 47, bottom - No.716 reverted to two bell shape which it carried from April 1943 to December 1945.**

(right) **The thirty built by Darlington all originally had one organ pipe on the right hand side, i.e. the driver's side, with a small bell-shape on the left-hand side.**

For some reason, those shedded at Haymarket had two bell shaped whistles so No.714 retained the first fitting. Haymarket, 4th August 1938.

729 cont./
SHEDS:
Gateshead.
York 21/2/25.
Neville Hill 20/11/26.
Tweedmouth 24/4/28.
Gateshead 20/3/39.
Darlington 28/3/43.
York 28/6/43.
Scarborough 12/3/45.

RENUMBERED:
Allocated **2962**.

CONDEMNED: 17/11/45.
Cut up at Darlington.

_____

732

N.B. Loco 19460.

To traffic 9/1911.

REPAIRS:
???. ?/?—?/11/14.**G.**
???. ?/?—?/12/19.**G.**
???. ?/?—22/11/22.**G.**
Ghd. 12/7—9/10/23.**G.**
Ghd. 28/2—22/3/24.**L.**
Ghd. 15/1—11/5/25.**G.**
Ghd. 17/2—10/3/26.**L.**
Ghd. 3/5—3/6/26.**G.**
Ghd. 25/11/26—8/3/27.**G.**
Ghd. 31/1—14/2/28.**L.**
Ghd. 16—25/5/28.**L.**
Ghd. 9/6—6/9/28.**G.**
Ghd. 23/9—29/11/29.**G.**
Ghd. 5—23/1/31.**L.**
Ghd. 30/6—21/8/31.**G.**
Ghd. 21—26/7/32.**N/C.**
Dar. 21/2—21/12/33.**G.**
Rebuilt to Part 2.
Dar. 4/3—3/4/35.**L.**
Dar. 28/5—19/7/35.**G.**
Dar. 29—31/7/35.**N/C.**
Dar. 25/3/36.*Weigh.*
Dar. 4/5/37.
Tender weigh.
Dar. 9/2—5/4/38.**G.**
Dar. 6—11/4/38.**N/C.**
Dar. 14—26/9/39.**N/C.**
Dar. 5/8—14/10/40.**G.**
Dar. 28/3—6/5/44.**G.**
Dar. 14/11/46. *Not repaired.*

BOILERS:
NBL 19460.
NBL 19454 *(ex720)* ?/11/14.
NBL 19448 *(ex718)* ?/12/19.
D1497 *(ex2205)* 8/3/27.
D1798 *(ex2196)* 29/11/29.
D1424 *(ex2209)* 21/8/31.
D1451 *(ex2208)* 21/12/33.
  2832 *(new)* 5/4/38.

SHEDS:
Gateshead.
York 2/2/34.
Scarborough 12/3/45.

RENUMBERED:
2963 10/11/46.

CONDEMNED: 14/12/46.
Cut up at Darlington.

_____

733

N.B. Loco 19461.

To traffic 10/1911.

REPAIRS:
???. ?/?—?/6/15.**G.**
???. ?/?—?/12/21.**G.**
???. ?/?—16/6/22.**G.**
Ghd. 25/4—25/7/23.**G.**
Ghd. 24/10/24—27/1/25.**G.**
Ghd. 2/7—10/11/26.**G.**
Ghd. 11/1—27/3/28.**G.**
Ghd. 23/8—23/10/29.**G.**
Dar. 19/12/30—5/1/31.**N/C.**
Ghd. 3/6—23/7/31.**G.**
Ghd. 13—18/7/32.**N/C.**
Dar. 7/2—2/3/33.
Tender only.
Dar. 31/1—9/3/34.**G.**
Westinghouse to Steam brake, &
screw reverse fitted.
Dar. 3/12/36—29/1/37.**G.**
Dar. 21/5—26/6/40.**G.**
Dar. 12/2—2/3/42.**L.**
Dar. 6/5—10/6/43.**G.**
Dar. 20/7/45. *Not repaired.*

BOILERS:
NBL 19461.
NBL 19453 *(ex719)* ?/6/15.
NBL 19447 *(ex719)* ?/12/21.
D1798 *(new)* 10/11/26.
  2060 *(new)* 27/3/28.
D792 *(ex714)* 23/7/31.
  2075 *(ex734)* 9/3/34.
D1505 *(exC6 703)* 29/1/37.
  2305 *(ex2210)* 26/6/40.
  2834 *(ex709)* 10/6/43.

SHEDS:
Gateshead.
Hull Dairycoates 28/3/43.

RENUMBERED:
Allocated **2964**.

CONDEMNED: 11/8/45.
Cut up at Darlington.

_____

734

N.B. Loco 19462.

To traffic 10/1911.

REPAIRS:
???. ?/?—?/9/15.**G.**
???. ?/?—?/4/18.**G.**
???. ?/?—?/3/20.**G.**
Ghd. 24/10/22—9/2/23.**G.**
Ghd. 31/3—12/7/24.**G.**
Ghd. 15—23/12/25.**L.**
Ghd. 27/4—14/9/26.**G.**
Ghd. 31/10—4/11/27.**L.**
Ghd. 13—20/12/27.**L.**
Ghd. 12/4—25/6/28.**G.**
Ghd. 21—25/3/29.
Tender only.
Ghd. 30/12/29—1/3/30.**G.**
Ghd. 16/2—29/3/32.**G.**
Westinghouse to Steam brake.
Ghd. 2—20/9/32.**L.**
Dar. 6/12/33—23/1/34.**G.**
Screw reverse fitted.
Dar. 31/3—11/6/36.**G.**
Dar. 21/8—3/9/36.**N/C.**
Dar. 10/7—25/8/39.**G.**
Dar. 29—31/8/39.**N/C.**
Dar. 10/11—6/12/41.**N/C.**
Dar. 9/4—12/5/42.**G.**
Dar. 10/11/42—4/1/43.**H.**
New cylinders.
Dar. 10/8/44. *Not repaired.*

BOILERS:
NBL 19462.
NBL 19458 *(ex728)* ?/9/15.
NBL 19455 *(ex721)* ?/4/18.
  D312 *(ex716)* ?/3/20.
  D463 *(ex2206)* 12/7/24.
D1799 *(ex719)* 25/6/28.
  2075 *(ex735)* 29/3/32.
  2462 *(new)* 23/1/34.
  2297 *(ex2166)* 25/8/39.
  2398 *(ex736)* 12/5/42.

SHEDS:
Gateshead.
Darlington 28/3/43.

RENUMBERED:
Allocated **2965**.

CONDEMNED: 16/9/44.
Cut up at Darlington.

_____

735

N.B. Loco 19463.

To traffic 10/1911.

REPAIRS:
???. ?/?—?/8/15.**G.**
???. ?/?—?/3/17.**G.**
???. ?/?—?/7/20.**G.**
???. ?/?—?/7/22.**G.**
Dar. 15/12/23—11/3/24.**G.**
Gresley snifter and
anti-carbonisers fitted.
Ghd. 2—14/10/25.**L.**
Ghd. 27/1—20/5/26.**G.**
Ghd. 28/7/26.**N/C.**
Ghd. 9—27/5/27.**L.**
Ghd. 29/11—10/12/27.**L.**
Ghd. 9/3—31/5/28.**G.**
Ghd. 30/1—18/3/30.**G.**
Ghd. 15/1—1/3/32.**G.**
Westinghouse to Steam brake.
Ghd. 11—17/3/32.**N/C.**
Dar. 18/1—23/2/34.**G.**
Screw reverse fitted.
Dar. 2/6—25/8/36.**G.**
Dar. 21/3—9/4/40.**N/C.**
After collision.
Dar. 31/12/40—8/2/41.**G.**
Dar. 19/3—27/4/43.**G.**
Dar. 30/4/43.**N/C.**
Dar. 8/12/44.*Weigh.*
Dar. 12/1/45.*Weigh.*
Dar. 1/6/45. *Not repaired.*

BOILERS:
NBL 19463.
NBL 19465 *(ex737)* ?/8/15.
NBL 19446 *(ex706)* ?/3/17.
NBL 19462 *(ex736)* ?/7/20.
NBL 19463 *(ex722)* ?/7/22.
  2075 *(new)* 31/5/28.
  2056 *(ex722)* 1/3/32.
  2402 *(ex2207)* 23/2/24.
  2464 *(ex2209)* 8/2/41.
  2583 *(ex2195)* 27/4/43.

SHEDS:
Gateshead.
Darlington 28/3/43.

RENUMBERED:
Allocated **2966**.

CONDEMNED: 16/6/45.
Cut up at Darlington.

_____

This stipulation meant a change from organ pipe to bell shape on the driver's side of No.2193.

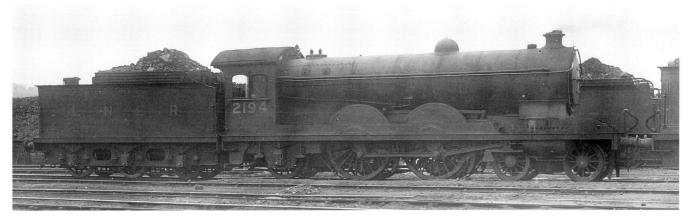

Likewise No.2194 had to have a bell shape on its right hand side instead of its original organ pipe. Haymarket, August 1935.

Although No.2205 was never at Haymarket in LNER years, it was at Tweedmouth from 9th June 1930, and worked regularly to the North, and was a ready reserve for any of the three Edinburgh engines. It too had its driver's organ pipe whistle replaced by a bell shape.

The last boilers built were the five in 1935 and another five in November 1936 and all ten only had a single whistle. This was mounted above an isolating valve on the firebox. Springhead.

Because the single whistle proved quite adequate, a number of those with twin mounting had their fitting changed. The organ pipe was discarded and replaced by the smaller bell shape, the pipe to the left-hand side then being blanked off. Cockburnspath Bank, 1946.

All fifty were first equipped with steam reversing gear which had two-handle control and this type was kept to 1930. Of the two handles in the cab one operated the rod alongside of the firebox and the crank down to the valve on the cataract cylinder of the gear. The other governed the steam supply from the boiler.

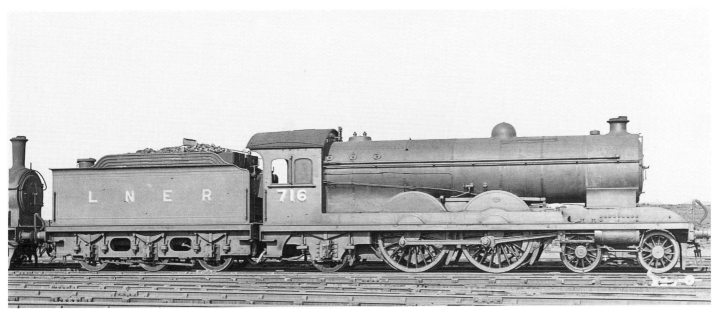

With the single handle type the steam control was moved from the cab to the outlet on the boiler, the valve being left open apart from when repair to the gear was needed. This enabled the rod and crank to be removed. At least nine, Nos.710, 716, 718, 2166, 2194, 2198, 2203, 2208 and 2209 are known to have been altered to single handle control and there may have been others. Darlington.

The second change was more radical in that the steam-operated reverse was altered to screw operated. No.721, ex works 3rd May 1933, was the first to be done and from October 1933 this was made standard for the whole class. No.720 was the last one with steam gear when it went into works on 1st July 1936.

Until the end of 1932 there were no sight screens on the cab sides.

736

N.B. Loco 19464.

To traffic 11/1911.

REPAIRS:
???. ?/?—?/10/15.**G.**
???. ?/?—?/8/20.**G.**
???. ?/?—30/8/22.**G.**
Ghd. 28/1—16/4/24.**G.**
Gresley snifter and
anti carbonisers fitted.
Ghd. 14—24/4/25.**L.**
Ghd. 4/12/25—26/3/26.**G.**
Dar. 23/5—9/9/27.**G.**
Ghd. 21—23/9/27.**N/C.**
Ghd. 10—11/10/27.**N/C.**
Dar. 12—17/10/27.**N/C.**
Ghd. 6/11—12/12/28.**L.**
Ghd. 7/5—17/7/29.**G.**
Ghd. 27/8—20/10/31.**L.**
Ghd. 5/4—19/5/32.**G.**
Westinghouse to Steam brake.
Dar. 1/5—4/6/34.**G.**
Screw reverse fitted.
Dar. 11/11/35—19/3/36.**G.**
Dar. 22/7—1/9/39.**G.**
Dar. 23/6—17/7/41.**L.**
Dar. 26/3—28/4/42.**G.**
Dar. 12/10/44.*Weigh.*
Dar. 30/3/46. *Not repaired.*

BOILERS:
NBL 19464.
NBL 19462 *(ex734)* ?/10/15.
NBL 19454 *(ex732)* ?/8/20.
D1651 *(new)* 26/3/26.
  D326 *(ex2199)* 9/9/27.
  2417 *(new)* 19/5/32.
D1651 *(ex2197)* 4/6/34.
  2398 *(ex2205)* 1/9/39.
D1651 *(ex2197)* 28/4/42.

SHEDS:
Gateshead.
Tweedmouth 25/4/28.
Gateshead 9/4/32.
Darlington 28/3/43.
Hull Dairycoates 20/12/44.

RENUMBERED:
Allocated **2967**.

CONDEMNED: 27/4/46.
Cut up at Darlington.

737

N.B. Loco 19465.

To traffic 12/1911.

REPAIRS:
???. ?/?—?/7/15.**G.**
???. ?/?—?/5/21.**G.**
Ghd. ?/?—17/10/22.**G.**
Ghd. 14/4—11/7/23.**G.**
Ghd. 5/1—9/4/25.**G.**
Ghd. 1/12/26—2/5/27.**H.**
Dar. 21/6—14/9/28.**G.**
Ghd. 11—17/12/28.**L.**
Ghd. 8/12/29—5/2/30.**G.**
Ghd. 2/6/31.**N/C.**
Tender only.
Ghd. 6/10—24/11/31.**G.**
Ghd. 20/10—5/12/32.**L.**
Dar. 1/10—3/11/34.**G.**
Westinghouse to Steam brake, &
screw reverse fitted.
Dar. 7/5—4/7/36.**G.**
Dar. 12/5—26/7/38.**G.**
Dar. 29/2—6/4/40.**N/C.**
Dar. 28/11—23/12/40.**N/C.**
Dar. 15/6—28/7/42.**G.**
Dar. 29/11/44—6/1/45.**G.**
Dar. 31/10/45. *Not repaired.*

BOILERS:
NBL 19465.
NBL 19451 *(ex717)* ?/7/15.
NBL 19452 *(ex727)* ?/5/21.
D1424 *(new)* 17/10/22.
  D462 *(exC6 696)* 2/5/27.
D1497 *(ex732)* 5/2/30.
  2057 *(exC6 532)* 3/11/34.
D1451 *(ex732)* 26/7/38.
  2841 *(exC6 703)* 28/7/42.
  2679 *(exC6 696)* 6/1/45.

SHEDS:
Gateshead.
York 3/12/31.
Scarborough 12/3/45.

RENUMBERED:
Allocated **2968**.

CONDEMNED: 22/12/45.
Cut up at Darlington.

2163

Darlington.

To traffic 5/1914.

REPAIRS:
???. ?/?—?/5/20.**G.**
???. ?/?—?/7/22.**G.**
Dar. 18/2—17/4/24.**G.**
Dar. 20/11/25—20/3/26.**G.**
Dabeg feed pump fitted.
Dar. 30/6—14/7/26.**L.**
Dar. 28/10—4/11/27.**L.**
Dar. 18/2—27/4/28.**G.**
Dar. 28/4—6/6/28.**N/C.**
Dar. 11/4—28/5/29.**H.**
Dar. 30/12/29—17/2/30.**G.**
Dar. 31/3—7/4/30.**N/C.**
Ghd. 18/12/31—7/1/32.**N/C.**
Brackets taken off for booster.
Dar. 17/3—20/5/32.**G.**
Westinghouse to Steam brake.
Different clack box.
Dar. 23/6—21/9/34.**G.**
Screw reverse fitted.
Dar. 4/3—8/5/36.**G.**
Dar. 20/1—1/3/37.**N/C.**
Dabeg taken off, & Exhaust
injector fitted.
Dar. 11/3—12/5/38.**G.**
Dar. 19/12/38—24/1/39.**N/C.**
Dar. 31/8—1/9/39.**N/C.**
Dar. 6—13/9/39.**N/C.**
Dar. 8/4—23/5/40.**N/C.**
Dar. 6/3—18/4/41.**G.**
Dar. 21—24/4/41.**N/C.**
Dar. 30/1—18/2/42.**G.**
Dar. 31/8—25/9/43.**G.**
Dar. 16/8—1/9/44.**L.**
Dar. 3/12/45. *Not repaired.*

BOILERS:
D315.
D338 *(ex2171)* ?/5/20.
D406 *(ex2195)* ?/7/22.
D851 *(exC6 1680)* 20/3/26.
D316 *(ex2165)* 27/4/28.
  2285 *(new)* 17/2/30.
  2461 *(ex2198)* 12/5/38.
  2428 *(ex719)* 18/4/41.
  2285 *(ex2203)* 25/9/43.

SHEDS:
York.
Tweedmouth 23/7/45.

RENUMBERED:
Allocated **2969**.

CONDEMNED: 8/1/46.
Cut up at Darlington.

2164

Darlington.

To traffic 5/1914.

REPAIRS:
???. ?/?—?/7/20.**G.**
Ghd. 12/6—14/9/23.**G.**
Dar. 17—22/9/23.**L.**
Dar. 21/12/23—22/2/24.**G.**
Dar. 26/8—24/11/25.**G.**
Dar. 1/12/27—27/2/28.**G.**
Dar. 17/9—20/12/28.**G.**
After Darlington collision.
Dar. 16/6—11/9/30.**G.**
Dar. 29/9—14/10/30.**N/C.**
Dar. 25/6—6/8/31.**L.**
Dar. 9/9—3/11/32.**G.**
Westinghouse to Steam brake.
Dar. 24/4—5/5/33.**N/C.**
Dar. 31/5—2/6/33.**N/C.**
Dar. 5/2—18/5/35.**G.**
Screw reverse fitted.
Dar. 3/3—16/4/37.**G.**
Dar. 19—30/4/37.**N/C.**
Dar. 5/1—9/2/39.**G.**
Dar. 27/9—6/11/41.**G.**
Dar. 12/5—10/6/44.**G.**
Dar. 6/4/46.*Weigh.*
Dar. 30/10/47—9/1/48.**G.**
Dar. 30/12/48. *Not repaired.*

BOILERS:
D316.
D315 *(ex2163)* ?/7/20.
D319 *(ex2166)* 22/2/24.
D342 *(ex2210)* 24/11/25.
  2335 *(new)* 11/9/30.
D1671 *(ex2165)* 18/5/35.
  2165 *(ex2199)* 16/4/37.
  2335 *(ex2165)* 9/2/39.
D1662 *(exC6 784)* 6/11/41.
  2577 *(exC6 295)* 10/6/44.
  2835 *(ex2974)* 9/1/48.

SHEDS:
York.
Tweedmouth 23/7/45.
Hull Dairycoates 26/10/47.

RENUMBERED:
2970 6/9/46.

CONDEMNED: 31/12/48.
Cut up at Darlington.

WORKS CODES:- Cw - Cowlairs. Dar- Darlington. Don - Doncaster. Ghd - Gateshead. Gor - Gorton. Inv - Inverurie. Nor - Norwich. Str - Stratford.
REPAIR CODES:- **C/H** - Casual Heavy. **C/L** - Casual Light. **G** - General. **H**- Heavy. **H/I** - Heavy Intermediate. **L** - Light. **L/I** - Light Intermediate. **N/C** - Non-Classified.

49

Ex works on 20th May 1932 No.2163 was the first to be fitted with vertical hinged triplex glass sight screen on each cab side between the windows. No.2198 was fitted from 14th March 1933 and the whole class was so equipped.

(above) Original smokebox door fastening was by a wheel and a handle and could still be seen on No.2172 (see page 41, bottom) until April 1936, although the change to two handles had begun before Grouping (see also page 34, top).

All duly acquired two handles for smokebox door fastening, the wheel having disappeared by 1936. One was last used on No.2169 in June 1934. York, 1934.

Until 1932 there were no lifting holes provided in the front end of the main frames.

As and when the engines went to Darlington works from 1932, lifting holes were drilled in the frame. No.2163 had them when ex works on 20th May 1932 (*see* page 63, bottom). York.

Until February 1929 all had North Eastern pattern drawhook, also taper shank buffers with solid spindle and circular flange.

Beginning with No.2203, ex works on 1st February 1929, there was then a steady change to the Group Standard buffers and drawhook. York.

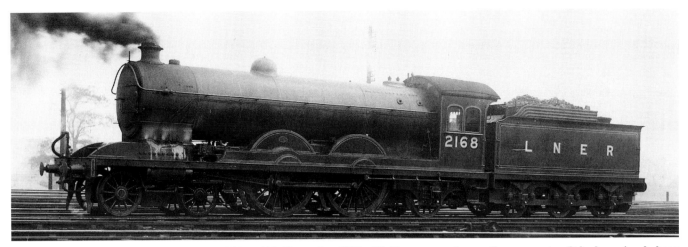

One engine, No.2168, ran from 19th May 1932 to 11th November 1935 with Flaman speed recording apparatus. It had previously been so fitted on 22nd March 1929.

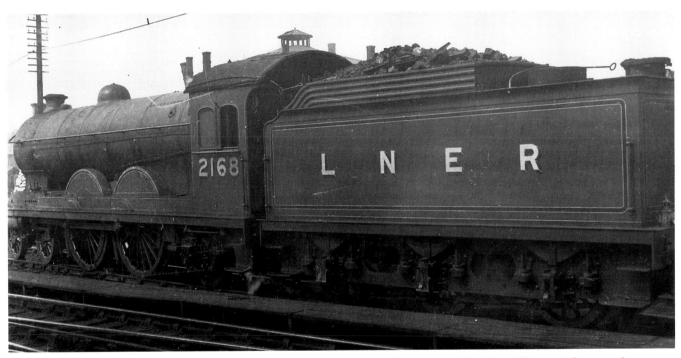

Before the Flaman speed recorder was taken off a section of the driving shaft was removed, so it would cease to be operative.

Until the end of October 1933 the whole class was fitted with Raven fog signalling apparatus. The striker can be seen just to the rear of the leading coupled wheel. Haymarket.

2165

Darlington.

To traffic 6/1914.

REPAIRS:
???. ?/?—?/9/20.**G.**
???. ?/?—?/12/22.**G.**
Dar. 15/1—2/2/23.**N/C.**
Dar. 21/12/23—15/3/24.**G.**
Gresley snifter fitted.
Dar. 25/11/25—11/6/26.**G.**
Dar. 25/1—19/4/28.**G.**
Ghd. 25—28/11/29.
Tender only.
Ghd. 6/1—28/2/30.**G.**
Ghd. 27—31/7/31.**L.**
Ghd. 6/5—20/6/32.**G.**
Westinghouse to Steam brake.
Dar. 4/2—23/4/35.**G.**
Screw reverse fitted.
Dar. 4/3/36.*Weigh.*
Dar. 29/12/38—3/2/39.**G.**
Dar. 6—21/2/39.**N/C.**
Dar. 3—3/10/39.**L.**
Dar. 22/6—6/8/42.**G.**
Dar. 17/1—16/2/46.**G.**
Dar. 20/6—15/7/46.**L.**
Dar. 12—16/12/46. *Not repaired
& sent to Gateshead.*
Dar. 28/12/46. *Not repaired.*

BOILERS:
D319.
D342 *(ex2172)* ?/9/20.
D316 *(ex2172)* ?/12/22.
D475 *(ex2203)* 19/4/28.
D1671 *(ex729)* 20/6/32.
2335 *(ex2164)* 23/4/35.
D1656 *(ex2202)* 3/2/39.
2578 *(ex2200)* 6/8/42.
2275 *(ex716)* 16/2/46.

SHEDS:
York.
Gateshead 10/5/29.
Tweedmouth 9/6/30.
Gateshead 28/3/42.
Darlington 28/3/43.
Hull Dairycoates 20/12/44.

RENUMBERED:
2971 10/11/46.

CONDEMNED: 1/2/47.
Cut up at Darlington.

2166

Darlington.

To traffic 6/1914.

REPAIRS:
???. ?/?—?/10/20.**G.**
Dar. 11—29/1/23.**L.**
Dar. 29/10/23—29/1/24.**G.**
Dar. 17/4—17/8/25.**G.**
Dar. 4—17/9/25.**L.**
Dar. 27/5—8/10/27.**G.**
Dar. 29/4—12/7/29.**G.**
Dar. 17/11/30—27/1/31.**G.**
Ghd. 23—30/3/31.**N/C.**
Dar. 28/4—8/5/31.**N/C.**
Dar. 24/4—15/6/33.**G.**
Westinghouse to Steam brake.
Dar. 14—25/8/33.**N/C.**
Dar. 30/3—31/5/35.**G.**
Screw reverse fitted.
Dar. 27/4—12/6/36.**L.**
Dar. 20/10/36—19/2/37.**G.**
Dar. 19/4—9/6/39.**G.**
Dar. 10—21/6/39.**N/C.**
Dar. 27/11/41—2/1/42.**G.**
Dar. 6/2—1/6/42.**H.**
New cylinders.
Dar. 27/9—4/11/44.**G.**
Dar. 13—20/11/44.**N/C.**
Dar. 17/4—17/5/47.**G.**
Dar. 2—4/6/47.**N/C.**
Dar. 19/8/48. *Not repaired.*

BOILERS:
D323.
D319 *(ex2165)* ?/10/20.
D429 *(ex2200)* 29/1/24.
D338 *(ex2207)* 8/10/27.
2396 *(new)* 27/1/31.
2280 *(ex2196)* 15/6/33.
D1615 *(ex721)* 31/5/35.
2297 *(ex719)* 19/2/37.
2459 *(ex2172)* 9/6/39.
2693 *(ex2206)* 2/1/42.
2420 *(exC6 742)* 17/5/47.

SHEDS:
York.
Neville Hill 2/2/34.
York 24/1/35.
Scarborough 26/11/45.

RENUMBERED:
2972 10/11/46.

CONDEMNED: 30/8/48.
Cut up at Darlington.

2167

Darlington.

To traffic 6/1914.

REPAIRS:
???. ?/?—?/5/21.**G.**
Dar. 10/2—15/5/23.**G.**
Dar. 17/1—22/4/25.**G.**
Dar. 13/7—30/11/26.**L.**
Dar. 13/6—30/8/28.**G.**
Dar. 24/2—6/3/29.**N/C.**
Dar. 5/5—14/8/30.**G.**
Dar. 8/2—5/4/32.**G.**
Westinghouse to Steam brake.
Dar. 5/2—21/3/34.**G.**
Screw reverse fitted.
Dar. 20/1—17/3/36.**G.**
Dar. 9/4—10/5/40.**G.**
Dar. 2/5—6/6/42.**G.**
Dar. 7/2—16/3/46.**G.**
Dar. 15/6/48. *Not repaired.*

BOILERS:
D326.
D332 *(ex2169)* ?/5/21.
D323 *(ex2168)* 22/4/25.
D547 *(exC6 1794)* 30/8/28.
2424 *(new)* 5/4/32.
2288 *(ex2168)* 17/3/36.
2417 *(ex2198)* 10/5/40.
2682 *(ex2212)* 6/6/42.
2578 *(ex2165)* 16/3/46.

SHEDS:
York.
Gateshead 7/5/34.
Darlington 28/3/43.
Hull Dairycoates 20/10/45.
York 26/11/45.
Heaton 29/9/46.
Scarborough 9/3/47.

RENUMBERED:
2973 24/11/46.

CONDEMNED: 26/6/48.
Cut up at Darlington.

2168

Darlington.

To traffic 6/1914.

REPAIRS:
???. ?/?—?/12/20.**G.**
Dar. 4/10/22—31/1/23.**G.**
Dar. 8/8—6/9/24.**L.**

Dar. 10/10/24—10/1/25.**G.**
Dar. 31/8—19/10/25.**L.**
Ghd. 26/5—9/8/27.**G.**
Dar. 17/1—22/3/29.**G.**
Flaman speed recorder fitted.
Ghd. 30/6—15/8/30.**G.**
Dar. 4—17/9/30.**N/C.**
Dar. 10/3—19/5/32.**G.**
Westinghouse to Steam brake.
Dar. 8/11—28/12/33.**G.**
Screw reverse fitted.
Dar. 11/11—27/12/35.**G.**
Speed recorder removed.
Dar. 18/2—17/7/36.**H.**
New cylinders.
Dar. 12/10—3/11/36.**N/C.**
Flaman recorder re-fitted.
Dar. 17/6—7/9/37.**L.**
Dar. 12/4—10/6/38.**G.**
Dar. 13—28/6/38.**N/C.**
Dar. 2/11—10/12/40.**G.**
Dar. 26/2—12/4/44.**G.**
Dar. 18/8/47. *Not repaired.*

BOILERS:
D330.
D323 *(ex2166)* ?/12/20.
D520 *(ex2211)* 10/1/25.
D1951 *(new)* 9/8/27.
D603 *(ex2201)* 15/8/30.
2288 *(exC6 1680)* 28/12/33.
2396 *(ex2202)* 27/12/35.
2419 *(ex710)* 10/6/38.
D1798 *(ex2201)* 10/12/40.
2835 *(ex721)* 12/4/44.

SHEDS:
York.
Hull Dairycoates 28/3/43.
York 26/11/45.
Heaton 29/9/46.

RENUMBERED:
2974 8/12/46.

CONDEMNED: 24/5/47.
Cut up at Darlington.

WORKS CODES:- Cw - Cowlairs. Dar- Darlington. Don - Doncaster. Ghd - Gateshead. Gor - Gorton. Inv - Inverurie. Nor - Norwich. Str - Stratford.
REPAIR CODES:- **C/H** - Casual Heavy. **C/L** - Casual Light. **G** - General. **H**- Heavy. **H/I** - Heavy Intermediate. **L** - Light. **L/I** - Light Intermediate. **N/C** - Non-Classified.

The Raven system was abandoned at the end of October 1933 and the engines quickly had their equipment taken off. Grantham.

In August 1932 No.717 was fitted with rail washing gear, the delivery pipe for which can be seen below the cab and to the rear of the carrying wheel. The official reason for fitting just one York based engine has not been found, but may have been due to use of the sanding gear causing interference with track circuits at the station.

2169

Darlington.

To traffic 6/1914.

REPAIRS:
???. ?/?—?/2/21.**G.**
Dar. 15/9/22—25/1/23.**G.**
Dar. 8/5—31/7/24.**G.**
Dar. 18/1—2/6/26.**G.**
Dar. 19/9—23/11/28.**G.**
Owen's regulator valve.
Ghd. 11—18/10/29.**N/C.**
Ghd. 29/10—5/11/29.**N/C.**
Dar. 28/3—13/6/30.**G.**
Dar. 24/2—18/4/32.**G.**
Westinghouse to Steam brake, &
Owen's regulator valve taken
off.
Dar. 23/11—5/12/32.**N/C.**
Dar. 2/6—7/7/34.**G.**
Screw reverse fitted.
Dar. 6/4—16/5/36.**G.**
Dar. 18—27/5/36.**N/C.**
Dar. 3/6—1/7/36.**N/C.**
Dar. 1/9—19/10/38.**G.**
Dar. 17/8—5/10/39.**L.**
Dar. 18/4—22/5/40.**G.**
Dar. 2/11—14/12/42.**G.**
Dar. 16—23/12/42.**N/C.**
Dar. 6/12/45—12/1/46.**G.**
Dar. 28/2—16/3/46.**L.**
Dar. 8/2—15/3/47.**L.**

BOILERS:
D332.
 D423 (ex2198) ?/2/21.
D1436 (ex2172) 31/7/24.
NBL 19458 (ex2172) 2/6/26.
 2144 (new) 23/11/28.
D1613 (ex2172) 18/4/32.
 D508 (ex714) 7/7/34.
 2330 (ex2207) 16/5/36.
 2285 (ex2163) 19/10/38.
D1957 (ex716) 22/5/40.
 2075 (ex2208) 14/12/42.
 2280 (exC6 697) 12/1/46.

SHEDS:
York.
Gateshead 10/12/28.
York 16/1/30.
Hull Dairycoates 28/3/43.
York 18/10/43.
Scarborough 23/12/46.

RENUMBERED:
2975 25/8/46.

CONDEMNED: 10/7/48.
Cut up at Darlington.

2170

Darlington.

To traffic 6/1914.

REPAIRS:
???. ?/?—?/1/21.**G.**
Dar. 9—19/6/23.**L.**
Ghd. 26/9—20/10/23.**L.**
Dar. 29/4—28/6/24.**G.**
Dar. 15/2—22/6/26.**G.**
Dar. 8/9—1/10/26.**L.**
Dar. 10/2—30/4/28.**H.**
Dar. 2—9/6/28.**N/C.**
Dar. 8—23/11/28.**H.**
Ghd. 20/11—4/12/29.**L.**
Dar. 17/3—28/5/30.**G.**
Ghd. 26/3/31.**N/C.**
Tender only.
Dar. 3/3—28/4/32.**G.**
Westinghouse to Steam brake, &
Owen's regulator valve.
Dar. 12/4—12/5/34.**G.**
Screw reverse fitted.
Dar. 21/4—10/6/36.**G.**
Dar. 13/7—5/8/37.**N/C.**
Dar. 15/12/37—18/2/38.**G.**
Dar. 1/5—5/6/40.**G.**
Dar. 21/7/43. *Not repaired.*

BOILERS:
D335.
D2037 (exC6 697) ?/1/21.
D1613 (new) 28/6/24.
D1473 (exC6 698) 30/4/28.
 2144 (ex2169) 28/4/32.
D1662 (exC6 1753) 12/5/34.
 2687 (ex2196) 18/2/38.
 2288 (ex2167) 5/6/40.

SHEDS:
Gateshead.
York 28/6/24.
Hull Dairycoates 28/3/43.

RENUMBERED:
Allocated **2976**.

CONDEMNED: 24/8/43.
Cut up at Darlington.

2171

Darlington.

To traffic 7/1914.

REPAIRS:
???. ?/?—?/3/20.**G.**
Dar. 16/10/23—5/1/24.**G.**
Dar. 17/4—30/7/25.**G.**
Dar. 17/8—3/9/25.**L.**
Dar. 6—29/10/25.**L.**

Dar. 16/8—31/10/27.**G.**
Dar. 2/4—12/6/29.**G.**
Dar. 9/2/31.
Rebuilt to Class C9.

BOILERS:
D338.
NBL 19449 (ex spare) ?/3/20.
D1586 (new) 5/1/24.

SHED:
York.

2172

Darlington.

To traffic 8/1914.

REPAIRS:
???. ?/?—?/8/20.**G.**
???. ?/?—?/10/22.**G.**
Dar. 27/3—19/6/24.**G.**
Dar. 18/2—8/6/26.**G.**
Dar. 26/3—9/6/28.**G.**
Dar. 27/9—10/10/29.**N/C.**
Dar. 28/1—5/4/30.**G.**
Ghd. 16—29/4/30.**N/C.**
Dar. 13/1—15/3/32.**G.**
Westinghouse to Steam brake.
Dar. 22—31/3/32.**N/C.**
Dar. 9/7—27/8/34.**G.**
Screw reverse fitted.
Dar. 30/8—13/9/34.**N/C.**
Dar. 29/4—9/7/36.**G.**
Dar. 18/8—12/10/36.**H.**
Dar. 2/3—22/4/39.**G.**
Dar. 11/4—22/5/42.**G.**
Dar. 6/11/44. *Not repaired.*

BOILERS:
D342.
 D316 (ex2164) ?/8/20.
D1436 (new) ?/10/22.
NBL 19458 (ex2197) 19/6/24.
 D449 (ex2204) 8/6/26.
D1613 (ex2170) 9/6/28.
 2420 (new) 15/3/32.
D1613 (ex2169) 27/8/34.
 2459 (ex2205) 9/7/36.
 2280 (ex721) 22/4/39.
 2297 (ex734) 22/5/42.

SHEDS:
York.
Hull Dairycoates 28/3/43.

RENUMBERED:
Allocated **2977**.

CONDEMNED: 2/12/44.
Cut up at Darlington.

2193

Darlington.

To traffic 12/1914.

REPAIRS:
Ghd. 1/11/22—28/2/23.**G.**
Ghd. 22/5—1/6/23.**L.**
Ghd. 27/2—18/3/24.**L.**
Ghd. 28/10/24—15/1/25.**G.**
Ghd. 7/6—7/9/27.**G.**
Ghd. 3—20/2/28.**L.**
Ghd. 13/2—8/5/29.**G.**
Ghd. 17/11—24/12/30.**G.**
Dar. 4/11—21/12/32.**G.**
Westinghouse to Steam brake.
Dar. 24/1—21/3/36.**G.**
Screw reverse fitted.
Dar. 7/11—29/12/39.**G.**
Dar. 19/2—27/3/42.**G.**
Dar. 15/8—14/9/44.**G.**
Dar. 13/8—15/9/45.**L.**
New cylinders.
Dar. 29/11/45.*Weigh.*
Dar. 24/6/46.*Weigh.*
Dar. 21/4/47.*Weigh.*
Dar. 11/8/48. *Not repaired.*

BOILERS:
D397.
 D508 (ex2209) 15/1/25.
 D332 (ex2208) 7/9/27.
D1637 (exC6 1753) 8/5/29.
D1951 (ex2168) 24/12/30.
 2298 (ex716) 21/12/32.
D1951 (exC6 697) 21/3/36.
 2427 (ex2195) 29/12/39.
 2283 (exC6 699) 27/3/42.
 2165 (exC6 699) 14/9/44.

SHEDS:
Haymarket.
St Margarets 17/4/43.
York 2/6/43.
Darlington 24/11/44.

RENUMBERED:
2978 24/11/46.

CONDEMNED: 30/8/48.
Cut up at Darlington.

2194

Darlington.

To traffic 12/1914.

REPAIRS:
Dar. 21/3—22/6/23.**G.**
Ghd. 17/12/24—25/3/25.**G.**
Ghd. 5/4—17/8/27.**G.**
Ghd. 3/6—16/8/29.**G.**

Although taken off in October 1933, the rail washing gear was put on again at the next general repair in January 1935. It was again removed, probably in April 1935. Sanding remained unaltered in points of application ahead of the leading and to the rear of the trailing coupled wheels. Whilst fitted with a Westinghouse pump, sanding was air operated, but was then changed to steam.

During 1938 experiments were made on fitting blackout screens for air raid precautions.

Until early 1924, cylinder lubrication was by a North Eastern pattern mechanical lubricator on the right hand running plate just behind the smokebox.

Beginning with No.735, ex works on 11th March 1924, the mechanical lubricator was taken off and replaced by a Detroit sight feed lubricator in the cab. York.

From the cab the four feed pipes were grouped together along the side of the boiler to the rear edge of the smokebox where they divided. One was led under the boiler and the other three went to the anticarboniser mounted on the smokebox saddle; all (except 2212) were so changed as they next went for repair.

Until the early 1930's axlebox lubrication was by an NER pattern mechanical lubricator on the left-hand main frame just behind the smokebox and there were oil boxes on each splasher for the horn cheeks.

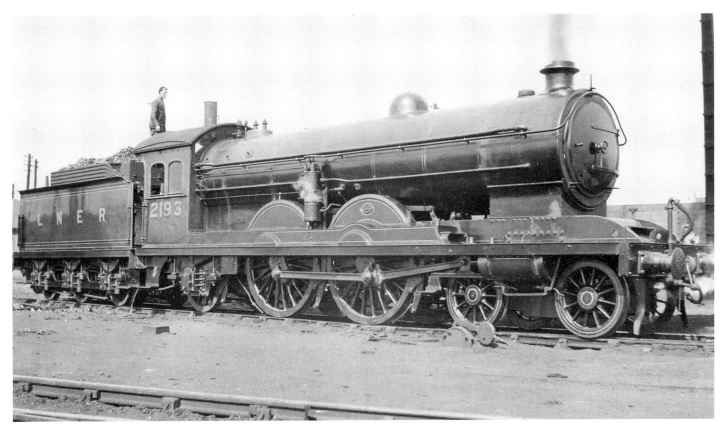

From 1924 when cylinder lubrication changed from mechanical to sight feed, there was no lubrication visible on the right hand side of the engine apart from the tallow cups to the slide bars.

Beginning with No.2204 on 31st March 1932 (No.2167 on 5th April 1932) the mechanical lubricator to the axleboxes was taken off and replaced by siphon lubrication from oil boxes in the cab, on both sides of the engine. Normanton shed, October 1936.

The siphon lubricator pipes ran diagonally down each side of the firebox to disappear behind the splashers. No.2206 was the last Part 1 engine to carry mechanical lubricator; it went to works on 16th August 1935. Gateshead, 1st April 1939.

During 1935, five engines Nos.2195 (February), 706 and 2165 (April), 2164 (May) and 2196 (September) had solid bronze axleboxes fitted, and these had Wakefield fountain lubricators in the cab with horizontal feed pipes to mid-way on the boiler.

2194 cont./
Ghd. 18—29/10/29.**L.**
Ghd. 9/2—19/3/31.**G.**
Dar. 24/5—14/7/33.**G.**
Westinghouse to Steam brake.
Dar. 3/4—30/5/36.**G.**
Screw reverse fitted.
Dar. 30/3—18/5/39.**G.**
Dar. 22—30/5/39.**N/C.**
Dar. 8/12/41—15/1/42.**G.**
Dar. 14/8/44. *Not repaired.*

BOILERS:
D403.
2398 *(new)* 19/3/31.
2060 *(exC6 699)* 30/5/36.
D1635 *(ex718)* 18/5/39.
2056 *(exC6 698)* 15/1/42.

SHEDS:
Haymarket.
Gateshead 16/3/39.
Darlington 28/3/43.
York 28/6/43.

RENUMBERED:
Allocated **2979**.

CONDEMNED: 2/9/44.
Cut up at Darlington.

2195

Darlington.

To traffic 12/1914.

REPAIRS:
???. ?/?—?/11/21.**G.**
Dar. 22/1—24/4/23.**G.**
Ghd. 28/5—20/8/24.**G.**
Ghd. 4/11/26—18/2/27.**G.**
Dar. 13/12/27—17/1/28.**L.**
Dar. 17/9—21/11/28.**G.**
Dar. 3/6—19/9/30.**G.**
Dar. 4/10—24/11/32.**G.**
Westinghouse to Steam brake.
Dar. 14/1—20/2/35.**G.**
Screw reverse fitted.
Dar. 31/7—4/9/35.**L.**
Dar. 18/11/35—12/5/36.**H.**
Dar. 10/11/37—20/1/38.**G.**
Dar. 21/1—3/2/38.**N/C.**
Dar. 28/1—1/3/39.**N/C.**
Dar. 8/11—21/12/39.**G.**
Dar. 13/5—3/6/40.**N/C.**
Dar. 26/5—10/6/42.**L.**
Dar. 26/2—7/4/43.**G.**
Dar. 23/11/46—4/1/47.**G.**
Dar. 10—18/1/47.**N/C.**
Dar. 28/1—6/2/47.**N/C.**
Dar. 7/5/47. *Not repaired.*

BOILERS:
D406.
D426 *(ex2199)* ?/11/21.
D477 *(ex2207)* 24/4/23.
D371 *(ex709)* 20/8/24.
2147 *(new)* 21/11/28.
D1456 *(ex2206)* 24/11/32.
2422 *(ex2210)* 20/2/35.
2427 *(ex2200)* 20/1/38.
2583 *(ex714)* 21/12/39.
2422 *(exC6 532)* 7/4/43.
2285 *(ex2163 & spare)* 4/1/47.

SHEDS:
Heaton.
York 27/12/24.
Hull Dairycoates 28/3/43.

RENUMBERED:
2980 4/1/47.

CONDEMNED: 28/6/47.
Cut up at Darlington.

2196

Darlington.

To traffic 2/1915.

REPAIRS:
Ghd. 18/6—27/9/23.**G.**
Gresley snifter and
anti carbonisers fitted.
Ghd. 8/4—17/7/25.**G.**
Ghd. 7—16/7/26.**L.**
Dar. 19/11—23/12/26.**L.**
Ghd. 31/1—25/3/27.**L.**
Ghd. 12/11/27—22/2/28.**G.**
Ghd. 11/9—31/10/29.**G.**
Ghd. 20/4—21/5/31.**G.**
Ghd. 1—12/6/31.**N/C.**
Painting & repairs to tender.
Dar. 2/3—21/4/33.**G.**
Westinghouse to Steam brake.
Dar. 3—22/5/33.**N/C.**
Dar. 12/12/33—7/2/34.**H.**
After collision
Screw reverse fitted..
Dar. 8/7—4/9/35.**G.**
After collision.
Dar. 7—28/10/35.**N/C.**
Dar. 16/11/37—22/1/38.**G.**
Dar. 14/2—1/4/41.**G.**
Dar. 20/2—10/7/42.**G.**
Dar. 3—29/6/44.**G.**
Dar. 17/6/48. *Not repaired.*

BOILERS:
D409.
NBL 19459 *(ex718)* 27/9/23.
D1798 *(ex733)* 22/2/28.
2280 *(new)* 31/10/29.
D1424 *(ex732)* 21/4/33.

2687 *(new)* 4/9/35.
D1637 *(ex2208)* 22/1/38.
2402 *(ex735)* 1/4/41.
2461 *(exC6 1794)* 29/6/44.

SHEDS:
Heaton.
York 4/7/38.
Hull Dairycoates 28/3/43.
Darlington 30/7/45.

RENUMBERED:
2981 22/12/46.

CONDEMNED: 9/7/48.
Cut up at Darlington.

2197

Darlington.

To traffic 2/1915.

REPAIRS:
Ghd. 21/2—16/5/23.**G.**
Dar. 4/3—30/5/24.**G.**
Gresley snifter &
Ramsbottom safety valves.
Ghd. 8/12/25—7/4/26.**G.**
Ghd. 21/11/27—14/2/28.**G.**
Ghd. 3—9/7/28.**L.**
Ghd. 28/12/28—4/1/29.**L.**
Ghd. 4/7—4/10/29.**G.**
Ghd. 2/4—17/6/31.**G.**
Ghd. 17—31/7/31.**L.**
Dar. 27/1—16/3/33.**H.**
Dar. 15/2—10/4/34.**G.**
Westinghouse to Steam brake, &
screw reverse fitted.
Dar. 14/7—5/9/36.**G.**
Dar. 25/6—22/9/37.**H.**
After collision.
Dar. 29/8—7/10/39.**G.**
Dar. 7/2—11/3/42.**G.**
Dar. 8/6—27/7/44.**G.**
Dar. 7/1—12/2/48.**G.**
Dar. 21/6/48. *Not repaired.*

BOILERS:
D418.
NBL 19458 *(exC6 703)* 16/5/23.
D2039 *(exC6 699)* 30/5/24.
D1662 *(new)* 7/4/26.
D1651 *(ex2207)* 17/6/31.
2578 *(new)* 10/4/34.
D1651 *(ex736)* 7/10/39.
2831 *(ex2199)* 11/3/42.
2402 *(ex2196)* 27/7/44.
2158 *(exC6 2931)* 12/2/48.

SHEDS:
Heaton.
York 27/12/24.
Heaton 8/2/25.

Tweedmouth 24/2/45.
Hull Dairycoates 26/10/47.

RENUMBERED:
2982 15/12/46.
E2982 12/2/48.

CONDEMNED: 24/7/48.
Cut up at Darlington.

2198

Darlington.

To traffic 3/1915.

REPAIRS:
???. ?/?—?/12/20.**G.**
Dar. 29/1—28/4/23.**G.**
Dar. 15/11—4/12/23.**L.**
Dar. 17/11—19/6/25.**G.**
Dar. 16/8—15/11/27.**G.**
Dar. 15/4—27/6/29.**G.**
Dar. 4/5—26/6/31.**G.**
Dar. 27/1—14/3/33.**G.**
Westinghouse to Steam brake.
Dar. 13/4/33.**N/C.**
Dar. 24/5—7/8/34.**L.**
Dar. 1/10—29/11/35.**G.**
Screw reverse fitted.
Dar. 5/3—7/4/36.**L.**
After collision.
Dar. 25/1—15/3/38.**G.**
Dar. 6—13/9/39.**N/C.**
Dar. 25/1—7/3/40.**G.**
Dar. 8—19/3/40.**N/C.**
Dar. 2—27/10/41.**N/C.**
Dar. 28/11—4/12/41.**N/C.**
Dar. 28/11/42—2/1/43.**G.**
Dar. 23/5—21/6/44.**L.**
After collision.
Dar. 27/11/45—19/1/46.**G.**
New cylinders.
Dar. 2/7/48. *Not repaired.*

BOILERS:
D423.
D2043 *(exC6 698)* ?/12/20.
D1456 *(new)* 28/4/23.
D429 *(ex2166)* 15/11/27.
D1586 *(ex2171)* 26/6/31.
D1430 *(ex710)* 14/3/33.
2461 *(ex2200)* 29/11/35.
2417 *(exC6 649)* 15/3/38.
D1951 *(ex2193)* 7/3/40.
D1957 *(ex2169)* 2/1/43.
2834 *(ex733)* 19/1/46.

SHEDS:
York.
Neville Hill 2/2/34.
York 18/7/34.
Hull Dairycoates 28/3/43.
York 18/10/43.

There was similar lubrication on both sides of the boiler. The pipes had inverted 'U' loops to avoid air locks. Nos.719 (January 1936) and 2169 (May 1936), got Fountain lubricators and similar piping, but those two retained normal brasses in their coupled axle boxes. Haymarket.

All were originally fitted with Westinghouse brake on the engine and for train brakes. Because they were designed for main line working they were also equipped with vacuum brake to suit ECJS stock on which that brake was standard. As was NER custom, the front-end brake connections were below the buffer beam.

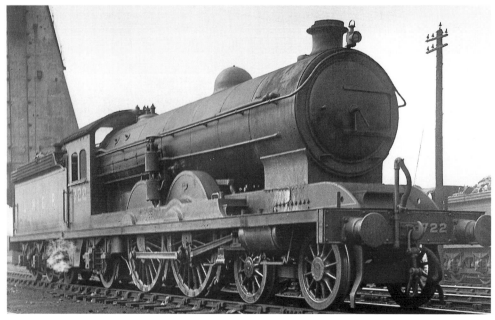

Beginning early in 1929 (*see* page 52, bottom), a swan-neck standpipe was put on for the front-end vacuum connection, but that for the air brake remained unaltered.

The engine brake was changed from Westinghouse to steam, in line with the Unification of Brakes programme. Starting with No.735, ex works on 1st March 1932, the Westinghouse pump and piping were taken off. No.719, to 30th April 1935, was the last to have Westinghouse. A minor addition from May 1934 (No.2170) was a small diameter drainpipe from the vacuum ejector exhaust pipe. Connection was inside the smokebox from which the drain emerged on the right hand side and then dropped down through the running plate to discharge on to the ballast.

(right) In January 1925 the GN Section began trials on Class O2 2-8-0 engine No.3500 of feed water heating on the Dabeg system. It was decided to try this on a mainline passenger engine and York C7 No.2163 was selected. On 20th March 1926, No.2163 was ex works fitted for Dabeg feed water heating. The pump was driven from the crank pin of the left hand rear coupled wheel, so did not work when the engine was standing which was a definite disadvantage. At first the clack box was on the side of the boiler just ahead of the firebox, but from 4th November 1927 was moved further forward. Note the temperature recorder on the side of the smokebox.

From 20th May 1932 the hot water entry to the boiler was altered to a top feed in front of the dome, but on 20th January 1937 the engine went to Darlington specially for the Dabeg apparatus to be taken off. York, August 1932.

When No.2163 was ex works on 1st March 1937, the Dabeg apparatus had been removed and a combined live and exhaust steam injector had been fitted. Doncaster.

During 1927, five sets of ACFI feed water-heating apparatus had been ordered, three of which went to Stratford and were put on B12 class engines. To widen the trial, two sets were sent to Darlington and, ex works on 26th January 1928, No.2206 carried one set. York.

The other set was used by No.728, ex works on 15th February 1928. The installation arrangement closely followed that on the B12 class, but on C7 class the exhaust from the Westinghouse pump went into the system to use its heat.

Apart from minor changes to the pipework, the ACFI apparatus continued in use on the two C7's until during the war.

2198 cont./
Tweedmouth 12/5/46.
Hull Dairycoates 26/10/47.

RENUMBERED:
2983 15/12/46.

CONDEMNED: 24/7/48.
Cut up at Darlington.

2199

Darlington.

To traffic 3/1915.

REPAIRS:
???. ?/?—?/8/21.**G.**
Dar. 9/3—23/6/23.**G.**
Dar. 17/12/24—9/4/25.**G.**
Dar. 17—27/4/25.**N/C.**
Dar. 10/2—20/6/27.**G.**
Dar. 5/10—2/11/27.**L.**
Dar. 15/2—19/4/29.**G.**
Dar. 13—27/6/30.**N/C.**
Dar. 28/4—19/6/31.**G.**
Dar. 17/1—7/3/33.**G.**
Westinghouse to Steam brake.
Dar. 12/11/34—26/1/35.**G.**
Screw reverse fitted.
Dar. 31/5—27/6/35.**L.**
Dar. 5/3—15/4/36.**L.**
After collision.
Dar. 8/2—20/3/37.**G.**
Dar. 22/11—1/12/38.**N/C.**
Dar. 27/2—1/5/39.**G.**
Dar. 20/6—3/7/39.**N/C.**
Dar. 7/1—7/2/42.**G.**
Dar. 7/6/44. *Not repaired.*

BOILERS:
D426.
 D326 *(ex2167)* ?/8/21.
D1953 *(new)* 20/6/27.
D1460 *(exC6 705)* 19/4/29.
D1953 *(ex2208)* 19/6/31.
 2158 *(ex718)* 7/3/33.
 2165 *(ex710)* 26/1/35.
 2831 *(new)* 20/3/37.
 2459 *(ex2166)* 7/2/42.

SHEDS:
York.
Hull Dairycoates 28/3/43.
York 13/5/44.

RENUMBERED:
Allocated **2984***.*

CONDEMNED: 24/6/44.
Cut up at Darlington.

2200

Darlington.

To traffic 3/1915.

REPAIRS:
Dar. 13/3—20/6/23.**G.**
Ghd. 20—29/2/24.**L.**
Ghd. 27/11/24—11/3/25.**G.**
Ghd. 3/9—1/10/26.**L.**
Ghd. 30/3—19/8/27.**G.**
Ghd. 6—30/11/28.**L.**
Ghd. 19/2—4/3/29.**L.**
Ghd. 4/4—6/6/29.**G.**
Ghd. 13—20/6/29.**L.**
Dar. 27/9—10/10/29.**N/C.**
Ghd. 13—25/3/30.**L.**
Ghd. 17/6—5/8/31.**G.**
Ghd. 28/8—9/9/31.**N/C.**
Dar. 15/9—1/11/33.**G.**
Westinghouse to Steam brake, &
screw reverse fitted.
Dar. 27/8—18/10/35.**G.**
Dar. 5/4—14/5/37.**G.**
Dar. 5—9/9/39.**N/C.**
Dar. 15/11—23/12/39.**G.**
Dar. 25/1—11/2/41.**N/C.**
Dar. 19/12/41—22/1/42.**G.**
Dar. 23/2—18/3/44.**G.**
Dar. 13/3/46. *Not repaired.*

BOILERS:
D429.
 D545 *(ex2210)* 20/6/23.
 D332 *(ex2193)* 6/6/29.
 2060 *(ex733)* 5/8/31.
 2461 *(new)* 1/11/33.
 2427 *(ex2206)* 18/10/35.
 2075 *(ex733)* 14/5/37.
 2578 *(ex2197)* 23/12/39.
D1635 *(ex2194)* 22/1/42.
 2432 *(ex710)* 18/3/44.

SHED:
Heaton.

RENUMBERED:
Allocated **2985***.*

CONDEMNED: 6/4/46.
Cut up at Darlington.

2201

Darlington.

To traffic 4/1915.

REPAIRS:
Dar. 18/3—18/6/24.**G.**
Dar. 28/1—24/6/26.**G.**
Ghd. 11/2—6/6/28.**G.**
Ghd. 17/10—23/12/29.**G.**

Ghd. 14/1—1/2/30.*Painted.*
Dar. 27/11—11/12/30.**N/C.**
Ghd. 25/8—25/9/31.**H.**
Ghd. 18—22/3/32.**N/C.**
Ghd. 20/6—12/8/32.**G.**
Westinghouse to Steam brake.
Dar. 3/10/34—9/2/35.**G.**
Screw reverse fitted.
Dar. 9/2—30/3/37.**G.**
Dar. 23/8—30/10/40.**G.**
Dar. 1—17/8/42.**N/C.**
Dar. 8—24/2/43.**N/C.**
Dar. 28/12/43—21/2/44.**G.**
Dar. 14/8/47. *Not repaired.*

BOILERS:
D430.
 D603 *(exC6 696)* 6/6/28.
 D515 *(ex2200)* 23/12/29.
D1798 *(ex732)* 25/9/31.
 D475 *(ex2165)* 12/8/32.
D1798 *(exC6 700)* 9/2/35.
 2298 *(exC6 702)* 30/10/40.
 2419 *(ex2209)* 21/2/44.

SHEDS:
Neville Hill.
Gateshead 8/2/28.
York 30/5/39.
Hull Dairycoates 28/3/43.

RENUMBERED:
2986 8/12/46.

CONDEMNED: 18/9/47.
Cut up at Darlington.

2202

Darlington.

To traffic 5/1915.

REPAIRS:
Dar. 12/12/22—24/3/23.**G.**
Dar. 5/7—8/10/24.**G.**
Dar. 30/12/25—10/6/26.**G.**
Dar. 7—27/7/26.**L.**
Ghd. 21/2—17/5/28.**G.**
Ghd. 9/5—31/7/29.**G.**
Ghd. 7—20/8/29.*Painted.*
Dar. 13/6—8/7/30.**N/C.**
Ghd. 29/5—3/6/31.**N/C.**
Ghd. 28/10—24/12/31.**G.**
Ghd. 20—22/4/32.**N/C.**
Dar. 7/2—2/3/33.
Tender only.
Dar. 7/9—13/10/33.**G.**
Westinghouse to Steam brake.
Dar. 9/10—22/11/35.**G.**
Screw reverse fitted.
Dar. 2/1—25/2/36.**L.**
Dar. 16/11—23/12/38.**G.**
Dar. 3/12/41—15/1/42.**G.**

Dar. 18/9/43. *Not repaired.*

BOILERS:
D435.
 D342 *(ex2165)* 24/3/23.
 D423 *(ex2169)* 8/10/24.
 D406 *(ex2163)* 10/6/26.
D1505 *(ex2209)* 31/7/29.
 2396 *(ex2166)* 13/10/33.
D1656 *(ex728)* 22/11/35.
 2330 *(ex2169)* 23/12/38.

SHEDS:
York.
Neville Hill 20/11/26.
Gateshead 8/2/28.
Tweedmouth 9/6/30.

RENUMBERED:
Allocated **2987***.*

CONDEMNED: 16/10/43.
Cut up at Darlington.

2203

Darlington.

To traffic 6/1915.

REPAIRS:
Ghd. 3/10/22—18/1/23.**G.**
Ghd. 5/5—13/8/24.**G.**
Dar. 9/6—4/9/25.**G.**
Dar. 9/7—19/10/27.**G.**
Ghd. 31/10—16/11/27.**L.**
Ghd. 23/11/28—1/2/29.**G.**
Dar. 13/6—9/7/29.**N/C.**
Ghd. 21/6—13/8/30.**G.**
Ghd. 28/10—18/11/31.**L.**
After collision with K2
No.4702 at Blaydon.
Dar. 3/1—22/2/33.**G.**
Westinghouse to Steam brake.
Dar. 26/6—23/8/35.**G.**
Screw reverse fitted.
Dar. 6—24/12/37.**N/C.**
Dar. 10/1—3/3/38.**G.**
Dar. 25/5—18/6/40.**G.**
Dar. 25/5—10/7/43.**G.**
Dar. 15/5—15/6/46.**G.**
Dar. 2/7/48. *Not repaired.*

BOILERS:
D446.
 D475 *(ex2208)* 4/9/25.
D1651 *(ex736)* 19/10/27.
 D315 *(ex spare)* 1/2/29.
 2464 *(new)* 22/2/33.
 2422 *(ex2195)* 3/3/38.
 2285 *(ex2169)* 18/6/40.
D1615 *(exC6 700)* 10/7/43.
 2682 *(ex2167)* 15/6/46.

Apart from losing the exhaust steam from the Westinghouse pump when the brake was changed to steam, No.728 (6th December 1932) and No.2206 (18th April 1932), there were no alterations on the right hand side. In November 1937 it was decided to dispense with all the ACFI feed water heating apparatus but both 728 and 2206 each survived another general repair before losing them, No.728 going to works on 2nd March 1940 and 2206 on 14th May 1941. Sheffield, Millhouses shed, July 1939.

On 27th June 1928 No.2164 was in collision with B16 No.2369 which had overrun signals when shunting at the south end of Darlington station. No.2164 was repaired and back in traffic on 20th December 1928. It had been returning from Scarborough on an excursion and was running at 45 m.p.h. under clear signals when it met 2369 head on.

No.2197 was working a return excursion from Scarborough on 14th June 1937 when its driver mis-read a signal at Newton Hall junction near Durham. Engine and tender were derailed and fell on to their sides but were back in traffic on 22nd September 1937.

In April 1921, No.2202 was fitted to burn oil on the Scarab system with its tender coal space taken by a 1240 gallon oil tank. The short coal rails were extended almost to the rear and given a downward sweep matching that at the front end. The trials were successful but the running cost per mile was double that of coal and the NER had coal owners on its Board!! The oil firing equipment was taken off in February 1922 and although stored, was never used again. The tender did however retain its longer than usual coal rails.

The tender with the long coal rails continued with No.2202 until 7th September 1933 when it was needing repair and was then removed from that engine. Ex works on 13th October 1933, No.2202 had the tender from Class Q6 0-8-0 No.2272 with similar but shorter coal rails.

After repair, the tender with the longer coal rails was put with No.732 at its rebuilding with Lentz valves and stayed with that engine from 21st December 1933 to withdrawal on 14th December 1946. Grantham.

2203 cont./
SHEDS:
Heaton.
Neville Hill 29/11/24.
Gateshead 8/2/28.
Tweedmouth 9/6/30.
York 3/8/39.
Hull Dairycoates 28/3/43.

RENUMBERED:
2988 22/12/46.

CONDEMNED: 24/7/48.
Cut up at Darlington.

_____

2204

Darlington.

To traffic 6/1915.

REPAIRS:
Ghd. 30/10/23—19/1/24.**G.**
Dar. 2/10—29/12/25.**G.**
Dar. 7/1—20/3/28.**G.**
Dar. 21/10—19/12/29.**G.**
Dar. 4/2—31/3/32.**G.**
Westinghouse to Steam brake.
Dar. 28/6—16/8/34.**G.**
Screw reverse fitted.
Dar. 27—30/8/34.**N/C.**
Dar. 27/12/34—4/2/35.**H.**
Dar. 10/6—21/8/36.**G.**
Dar. 27/8—14/9/36.**N/C.**
Dar. 2/12/38—28/1/39.**G.**
Dar. 30/1—1/2/39.**N/C.**
Dar. 8—21/2/39.**N/C.**
Dar. 24/2—13/3/39.**N/C.**
Dar. 30/9—27/11/41.**G.**
Dar. 7/6—1/7/44.**G.**
Dar. 20/6—9/8/47.**G.**
Dar. 3—11/9/47.**L.**
Dar. 18/8/48. *Not repaired.*

BOILERS:
D449.
D446 *(ex2203)* 29/12/25.
D330 *(ex706)* 19/12/29.
2144 *(ex2170)* 16/8/34.
2679 *(ex722)* 28/1/39.
2335 *(ex2164)* 27/11/41.
2462 *(ex718)* 1/7/44.
2285 *(ex2980)* 9/8/47.

SHEDS:
Haymarket.
Gateshead 1/3/23.
York 23/4/24.
Hull Dairycoates 28/3/43.
York 13/5/44.
Scarborough 26/11/45.

RENUMBERED:
2989 22/12/46.

CONDEMNED: 30/8/48.
Cut up at Darlington.

_____

2205

Darlington.

To traffic 11/1916.

REPAIRS:
Dar. 8/3—7/7/23.**G.**
Dar. 10/9—20/10/23.**H.**
Ghd. 9/1—26/3/25.**G.**
Ghd. 17/8—5/11/26.**G.**
Ghd. 28/4—12/7/28.**G.**
Dar. 13/3—8/8/29.**G.**
Dar. 29/8—13/9/29.**N/C.**
Dar. 26/10—13/11/29.**H.**
Ghd. 4/5—12/6/31.**G.**
Dar. 1/3—13/4/33.**G.**
Westinghouse to Steam brake.
Dar. 15/4—12/6/36.**G.**
Screw reverse fitted.
Dar. 3/6—27/7/39.**G.**
Dar. 21/1—25/3/43.**G.**
Dar. 2/2/45. *Not repaired.*

BOILERS:
D459.
NBL 19456 *(ex706)* 7/7/23
D1497 *(new)* 20/10/23.
D426 *(ex706)* 5/11/26.
2459 *(new)* 13/4/33.
2398 *(ex2194)* 12/6/36.
2060 *(ex2194)* 27/7/39.

SHEDS:
Gateshead.
Tweedmouth 9/6/30.

RENUMBERED:
Allocated **2990**.

CONDEMNED: 17/2/45.
Cut up at Darlington.

_____

2206

Darlington.

To traffic 11/1916.

REPAIRS:
???. ?/?—16/6/22.**G.**
Ghd. 4/10—10/12/23.**G.**
Dar. 17/4—20/8/25.**G.**
Dar. 28/8—10/9/25.**N/C.**
Dar. 28/9/27—2/1/28.**G.**
A.C.F.I. fitted.
Dar. 2—3/2/28.**N/C.**
Dar. 20/2—25/3/29.**N/C.**
Dar. 1/10—3/12/29.**G.**
Dar. 21/5—5/6/30.**L.**

Dar. 30/7—7/8/30.**N/C.**
Dar. 3—25/2/31.**N/C.**
Ghd. 29/5—9/6/31.**N/C.**
Dar. 15/2—18/4/32.**G.**
Westinghouse to Steam brake.
Dar. 22/8—1/9/33.**N/C.**
Dar. 16/8—2/10/35.**G.**
Screw reverse fitted.
Dar. 11/11/38—4/1/39.**G.**
Dar. 14/5—26/6/41.**L.**
A.C.F.I. removed.
Dar. 9/10—29/11/41.**G.**
Dar. 1/8—9/9/44.**G.**
Dar. 17/10/47. *Not repaired.*

BOILERS:
D463.
D310 *(exC6 704)* 10/12/23.
D1456 *(ex2198)* 26/1/28.
2427 *(new)* 18/4/32.
D1424 *(ex2196)* 2/10/35.
2693 *(ex728)* 4/1/39.
2396 *(ex2211)* 29/11/41.
D1613 *(ex2211)* 9/9/44.

SHEDS:
Heaton.
Neville Hill 29/11/24.
York 27/8/25.
Neville Hill 20/11/26.
Gateshead 8/2/28.
York 2/6/28.
Hull Dairycoates 28/3/43.
York 13/5/44.
Heaton 12/5/46.

RENUMBERED:
2991 14/1/47.

CONDEMNED: 8/11/47.
Cut up at Darlington.

_____

2207

Darlington.

To traffic 1/1917.

REPAIRS:
Dar. 4/12/22—19/2/23.**G.**
Dar. 19/11/24—20/3/25.**G.**
Dar. 8—30/6/25.**N/C.**
Painted for Centenary exhibition.
Dar. 30/3—29/6/27.**G.**
Ghd. 14/12/28—20/3/29.**G.**
Ghd. 8/4—6/5/29.**L.**
Ghd. 29/4—23/5/30.**H.**
Ghd. 10/3—4/5/31.**G.**
Ghd. 20—27/5/31.**N/C.**
Dar. 22/12/33—2/2/34.**G.**
Westinghouse to Steam brake, & screw reverse fitted.
Dar. 11/3—6/5/36.**G.**

Dar. 5—22/4/37.**N/C.**
Dar. 21/4—11/6/38.**G.**
Dar. 3/10—19/12/38.**H.**
Dar. 9—20/12/40.
Tender only.
Dar. 9/6—31/7/41.**G.**
Dar. 15/2—22/3/44.**G.**
Dar. 10/8—7/9/46.**L.**
Dar. 24/2—19/4/47.**G.**
Dar. 10—20/6/47.**N/C.**
Dar. 4/10/48. *Not repaired.*

BOILERS:
D477.
D338 *(ex2163)* 19/2/23.
D312 *(ex706)* 29/6/27.
D1651 *(ex2203)* 20/3/29.
2402 *(new)* 4/5/31.
2330 *(exC6 703)* 2/2/34.
2424 *(ex2167)* 6/5/36.
2421 *(ex729)* 11/6/38.
2424 *(ex722)* 31/7/41.
2275 *(ex2971)* 19/4/47.

SHEDS:
Neville Hill.
Tweedmouth 8/2/28.
York 10/9/38.
Hull Dairycoates 28/3/43.
Scarborough 5/3/45.

RENUMBERED:
2992 22/12/46.

CONDEMNED: 1/11/48.
Cut up at Darlington.

_____

2208

Darlington.

To traffic 2/1917.

REPAIRS:
Dar. 14/9—5/10/23.**L.**
Dar. 28/3—20/6/24.**G.**
Dar. 4/5—6/8/25.**G.**
Ghd. 20/4—17/8/27.**G.**
Dar. 26/2—30/4/29.**G.**
Dar. 14/4—17/6/31.**G.**
Dar. 29/6—21/8/33.**G.**
Westinghouse to Steam brake.
Dar. 8/5—21/8/35.**G.**
Screw reverse fitted.
Dar. 16/8—1/10/37.**G.**
Dar. 8—15/10/37.**N/C.**
Dar. 23/5—30/6/38.**H.**
Dar. 9/2—20/3/39.**N/C.**
Dar. 29/11/39—12/1/40.**G.**
Dar. 13/10—18/11/42.**G.**
Dar. 30/12/44—2/1/45.*Weigh.*
Dar. 14/8—22/9/45.**G.**
Dar. 19/2/48. *Not repaired.*

The twenty engines built in 1911 had the current NER standard tender carrying 5 tons of coal and 4125 gallons of water. There were three coal rails along the full length of each side and across the back with a fourth rail around the coal space, plated on the inside. The frame slots had horizontal base and almost hemispherical shape. Near Beningborough.

Nos.2163 to 2172 had similar tenders for capacity and coal rail arrangement but differed in the shape of the frame slots. These were now straight top and bottom with almost semi-circular ends.

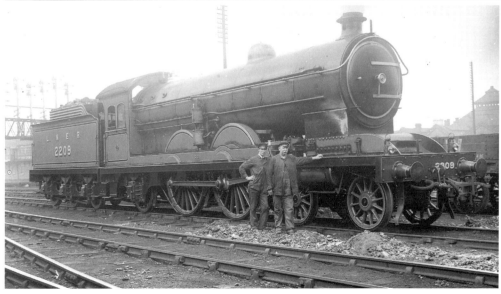

The tenders built for Nos.2193 to 2211 were re-designed. Water capacity was still 4125 gallons but 5$\frac{1}{2}$ tons of coal could be carried and the bunker sides and back plate were sloped to make it self-trimming. The three coal rails at each side now stopped short at the rear of the coal space. York.

In June 1928 the self-trimming tenders were removed from Nos.2208 and 2209 and replaced by the earlier type from Nos.2168 and 2167 respectively. The latter pair had their tenders renumbered as shown. York, July 1928.

Nos.2167 and 2168 required the ½ ton extra coal capacity because they were York shed's reserve engines to cover any hitch on the running of the non-stop *FLYING SCOTSMAN* train. Gateshead (Greensfield), 2nd August 1936.

(below) Early in 1932 a York driver suggested that self trimming tenders built from 1917 for and running with Q6 class could be better utilised put with C7 class where the tender did not have that facility. This was accepted so in 1933 Nos.2208 and 2209 again had self-trimming tenders coupled to them.

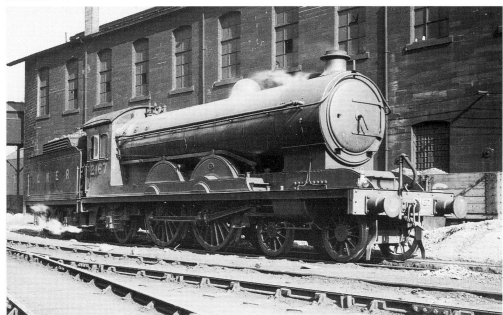

The older tenders from Q6 class built April to December 1917, although self-trimming, were the type with the coal rails cut short. In June 1933 No.2166 got the tender from No.2220 and others to get this type were Nos.710, 714, 717, 718, 722, 737, 2165, 2169, 2172 and 2208.

Class Q6 tenders built from August 1918 had rails curved down at the rear and eighteen of these were taken for the exchange with C7 class. In February 1937 a change to one of these was made on No.2166.

The contractor-built engines arrived fitted with the maker's circular type works numberplate on the smokebox saddle, but the NER very soon took them off.

Standard livery until 1923 was NER green with lining and 24in. wide brass number plate. The large company armorial was carried on the tender and the smaller circular version on the rear splasher. Buffer beam numbering was 6in. deep plus 1in. of shading. This NER painting continued at Gateshead to the end of February on No.716 (23rd February), 718 (15th February), 721 (15th February), 734 (9th February), 2193 (28th February), 2203 (18th January) and 2211 (1st February). From Darlington, No.2202 (24th March) also had it, and from there on 31st January 1923 No.2168 came out with 6in. N.E.R. above 12in. numbers on its tender but still with large brass plate on cab side.

2208 cont./
BOILERS:
D475.
D332 (ex2167) 6/8/25.
D508 (ex2193) 17/8/27.
D1953 (ex2199) 30/4/29.
D1451 (ex727) 17/6/31.
D1637 (exC6 649) 21/8/33.
2418 (ex2210) 1/10/37.
2075 (ex2200) 12/1/40.
2417 (ex2167) 18/11/42.
2841 (ex737) 22/9/45.

SHEDS:
York.
Hull Dairycoates 28/3/43.
York 13/5/44.
Scarborough 26/11/45.

RENUMBERED:
2993 8/12/46.

CONDEMNED: 6/3/48.
Cut up at Darlington.

_____

2209

Darlington.

To traffic 4/1917.

REPAIRS:
???. ?/?—6/7/22.G.
Ghd. 13/8—7/9/23.L.
Ghd. 7/1—14/3/24.G.
Ghd. 21/4—29/7/25.G.
Ghd. 13/5—1/9/27.G.
Ghd. 13—16/9/27.L.
Dar. 21/6—11/7/28.L.
Ghd. 8/4—24/6/29.G.
Ghd. 19/2—2/4/31.G.
Ghd. 30/4—11/5/31.Painted.
Ghd. 20—28/5/31.N/C.
Dar. 10—17/7/31.N/C.
Dar. 21/4—31/5/33.G.
Westinghouse to Steam brake.
Dar. 20—28/6/33.N/C.
Dar. 19/12/33—8/2/34.H.
After collision.
Dar. 5/7—15/8/34.L.
After collision.
Dar. 5/9—15/12/35.G.
Screw reverse fitted.
Dar. 7/2—23/3/38.G.
Dar. 4/11—17/12/40.G.
Dar. 14/1/44. Not repaired.

BOILERS:
D508.
D1505 (new) 14/3/24.
D1424 (ex720) 24/6/29.
D1598 (exC6 649) 2/4/31.
D1953 (ex2199) 31/5/33.

2464 (ex2203) 23/3/38.
2419 (ex2168) 17/12/40.

SHEDS:
Gateshead.
Heaton 21/2/25.
York 4/7/38.
Hull Dairycoates 28/3/43.

RENUMBERED:
Allocated 2994.

CONDEMNED: 5/2/44.
Cut up at Darlington.

_____

2210

Darlington.

To traffic 5/1917.

REPAIRS:
Dar. 17/2—18/5/23.G.
Dar. 24/9—10/12/24.L.
Dar. 24/3—21/5/25.G.
Dar. 18/2—12/7/27.G.
Dar. 4/6—15/8/29.G.
Ghd. 15/1—10/2/31.L.
Ghd. 15/5—8/7/31.G.
Dar. 21/2—11/4/33.G.
Westinghouse to Steam brake.
Dar. 10/12/34—13/2/35.G.
Screw reverse fitted.
Dar. 17/2—8/4/37.G.
Dar. 30/1—26/7/40.G.
Dar. 2/5—18/6/42.L.
Dar. 10/4—13/5/43.G.
Dar. 14/9—20/10/45.G.
Dar. 10—21/2/47.
Sent to Gateshead.
Ghd. 24/2—4/6/47.L.
Dar. 18/6/48. Not repaired.

BOILERS:
D515.
D435 (ex2202) 18/5/23.
D342 (ex2202) 10/12/24.
D435 (ex spare) 21/5/25.
2422 (new) 11/4/33.
2418 (ex2212) 13/2/35.
2305 (exC6 295) 8/4/37.
2687 (ex2170) 26/7/40.
2464 (ex735) 13/5/43.
2417 (ex2208) 20/10/45.

SHEDS:
Neville Hill.
Heaton 28/6/29.
Tweedmouth 21/11/43.
Hull Dairycoates 26/10/47.

RENUMBERED:
2995 22/12/46.

CONDEMNED: 9/7/48.
Cut up at Darlington.

_____

2211

Darlington.

To traffic 6/1917.

REPAIRS:
Ghd. 18/10/22—1/2/23.G.
Dar. 11/6—11/9/24.G.
Ghd. 28/10/26—16/2/27.G.
Ghd. 15/6—7/7/27.L.
Ghd. 24/5—17/8/28.G.
Ghd. 22/3—12/4/29.L.
Ghd. 20/12/29—13/2/30.G.
Ghd. 1/3—15/4/32.G.
Westinghouse to Steam brake.
Dar. 12/9—31/10/33.G.
Screw reverse fitted.
Dar. 22/11—21/12/33.N/C.
Dar. 18/11/35—16/1/36.G.
Dar. 19/5—27/7/38.G.
Dar. 1/10—15/11/41.G.
Dar. 13—22/1/43.N/C.
Dar. 4/7—16/8/44.G.
Dar. 24/10/47. Not repaired.

BOILERS:
D520.
D532 (exC6 1794) 11/9/24.
D462 (ex737) 13/2/30.
2428 (new) 15/4/32.
2283 (exC6 698) 16/1/36.
2396 (ex2168) 27/7/38.
D1613 (ex717) 15/11/41.
2831 (ex2197) 16/8/44.

SHEDS:
Heaton.
York 27/12/24.
Heaton 12/2/25.
Alston 29/5/40.
Gateshead 2/11/40.
Hull Dairycoates 28/3/43.
Scarborough 5/3/45.
Heaton 29/9/46.

RENUMBERED:
2996 8/12/46.

CONDEMNED: 8/11/47.
Cut up at Darlington.

_____

2212

Darlington.

To traffic 6/1918
with "Uniflow" cylinders.

REPAIRS:
Ghd. 15/10/22—22/3/23.G.
Ghd. 12—14/9/23.N/C.
Ghd. 2/12/24—23/3/25.G.
Ghd. 14/7—3/9/26.L.
Ghd. 12/1—20/4/28.G.
Dar. 2—12/6/28.N/C.
Ghd. 6/6—19/7/29.L.
Ghd. 18/1—25/3/30.G.
Ghd. 30/5—20/7/32.G.
Westinghouse to Steam brake.
Dar. 1/11—1/12/33.L.
Dar. 21/11/34—14/1/36.G.
Rebuilt to Part 2.
Dar. 20/1—8/2/36.N/C.
Dar. 17/1—10/3/39.G.
Dar. 17/1—14/3/40.L.
Dar. 16/8—3/9/40.L.
Dar. 17/3—5/5/42.G.
Dar. 25/9/45. Not repaired.

BOILERS:
D603.
D477 (ex2195) 23/3/25.
2418 (new) 20/7/32.
2682 (new) 14/1/36.
2057 (ex721) 5/5/42.

SHEDS:
Gateshead.
York 29/5/39.
Hull Dairycoates 28/3/43.
York 18/10/43.

RENUMBERED:
Allocated 2997.

CONDEMNED: 16/10/45.
Cut up at Darlington.

_____

To help the LNER Directors choose Group liveries, on 25th January 1923 Darlington turned out No.2169 in NER green with large brass numberplate but no armorial on the splasher. The tender carried 6in. L.&N.E.R. over 12in. numbers. On 19th February 1923, No.2207 appeared in GNR green with small numberplate on the cab but with the tender in the same style as 2169; both these had 6in. numbers at the front. No.2195 (24th April 1923) was first in this style followed from Darlington by 2198 (28th April), 722 (30th April), 2167 (15th May), 2210 (18th May), 706 (30th May) and 714 (31st May) and from Gateshead 2197 (16th May); all had 4$\frac{1}{2}$in. numbers at the front. The full points were then dropped and the lettering became the standard 7$\frac{1}{2}$in. From Darlington 2200 (20th June), 2194 (22nd June), 2199 (23rd June), 2205 (7th July) and from Gateshead 727 (5th July), 737 (11th July) and 733 (25th July) got the style shown here. The ampersand was then discarded but before area suffix D was introduced only LNER 720, ex Gateshead on 20th August 1923, was turned out.

(centre) This 'freak' L&NER 2205D arose because the engine was out with L&NER from general repair on 7th July 1923 but was in Darlington again from 10th September to 20th October 1923 and when then ex works the suffix had been added.

The area suffix was used from September 1923 to the end of January 1924. In addition to No.2205 described above it was applied to 2164 (14th September), 2196 (27th September), 719 (28th September), 732 (9th October), 2206 (10th December), and in 1924:- 2171 (5th January), 709 (17th January), 2204 (19th January) and 2166 (29th January). Sheffield (Victoria).

The other twenty two went straight from NER to LNER standard livery: in 1924 No.735 (11th March), 2209 (14th March), 2165 (15th March), 728 (8th April), 736 (16th April), 2163 (17th April), 729 (14th June), 721 (14th June), 2201 (18th June), 2172 (19th June), 2208 (20th June), 2170 (28th June), 734 (12th July), 718 (25th July), 710 (25th July), 716 (6th August), 717 (7th August), 2203 (13th August), 2211 (11th September), 2202 (8th October), and finally 2168 on 10th January 1925 and 2193 on 15th January 1925. Those in the various styles done previously acquired the standard when next they went for repair.

This was a Darlington painted engine because they put a white lining panel on each end of the wood sandwich front buffer beam. York.

Gateshead painted engines had no lining on the ends of the buffer beam. They were left black to match the angle of the running plate.

From March 1929 the number was moved from tender to cab side but it was another three years before Class C7 was used instead of Z on the front buffer beam.

(below) Moving the number to the cab enabled 12in. LNER to be on the tender. It also facilitated the exchange of tenders where this could be done to advantage. Green livery continued to be applied to November 1941 and six early withdrawals kept it. These were Nos.710, 714, 717, 719, 2170 and 2209.

In 1942 unlined black was put on to Nos.721 (18th April), 728 (4th April), 734 (12th May), 736 (28th April), 2163 (18th February), 2167 (6th June), 2194 (15th January), 2199 (7th February) and 2202 (15th January) and these still had LNER on the tender which they kept to withdrawal. No.2167 was unusual in keeping LNER and never having just NE on tender. After being the last to get LNER on 6th June 1942 it was not ex works again until 16th March 1946 by which time LNER was being restored. No.2167 changed to 2973 on 24th November 1946. Seven others Nos. 2166 (2nd January 1942), 2193 (17th March 1942), 2197 (11th March 1942), 2200 (22nd January 1942), 2204 (27th November 1941), 2206 (29th November 1941) and 2211 (15th November 1941) also got LNER on black but all had general repairs during 1944 when it became only NE.

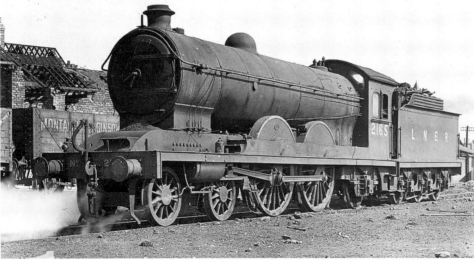

(above) Starting in 1942 with Nos.2196 (10th July), 737 (28th July) and 2165 (6th August) only NE was used on the tender of all those shopped until 12th January 1946 when No.2169 was ex works still with only NE as was 2198 on 19th January 1946.

(left) Only three No.716 ex works on 9th February 1946 and 2165 out on 16th February 1946 had LNER restored in shaded transfers but 2167, out 16th March 1946, had never lost them. The third to get them was 2203 out on 15th June 1946.

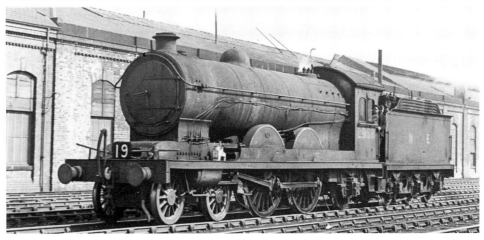

During 1946 the survivors were renumbered, all except 722/2960 and 2195/2980 at their home shed. No.720 changed to 2958 on Sunday 31st March 1946 at Scarborough, the local painter attempting block numbers but unshaded and this was the style which was generally adopted (but see page 81, top, for an exception). Hull, 17th April 1947.

(above) **By the end of 1946, Darlington had ceased to apply transfers and were painting numbers and letters in yellow unshaded Gill sans but with modified 9's. Nos.2980 (4th January 1947), 2992 (19th April 1947), 2972 (17th May 1947), 2989 (9th August 1947) and 2970 (9th January 1948) were the five to get this style. York, October 1948.**

(centre) **No.2982 had been changed from 2197 on Sunday 15th December 1946 at its home shed of Tweedmouth in the style used by local painters. St Margarets, July 1947.**

No.2975 renumbered from 2169 at York shed on Sunday 25th August 1946 was a typical example of the state of neglect accorded this class in 1946-1948.

(above) No.722 became 2960 whilst it was in Darlington works from 2nd to 27th March 1946 hence its acquisition of shaded transfers. Neville Hill shed, June 1946.

No.2970 was the last C7 to get LNER painting and was not ex works until 9th January 1948. York, October 1948.

Only one acquired British Railways painting, No.E2982, ex works on 12th February 1948, during the brief nine weeks when a regional prefix was being put on.

When No.2193 became 2978 on Sunday 24th November 1946 it was at Darlington shed and the job was done in shaded figures clearly by a works painter.

Throughout, No.2212 differed from any other C7 but neither the NER nor the LNER classified it separately. Built in June 1918 it had 'Uniflow' cylinders, and its tender did not have cut-off coal rails.

It changed to LNER livery on 23rd March 1925 but kept its Wakefield mechanical lubricator for the front end. The striker for the Raven fog apparatus can be seen just behind the leading coupled wheel. The major difference was in the cylinders where the steam flow was only in one direction. The consequent double length of the cylinders needed bogie wheels of 3ft 1¼in. in place of 3ft 7¼in. and a wheelbase 6in longer at 7ft 0in. Although it started with two handles on the smokebox door, one was soon changed to a wheel and it had the Gresley anti-vacuum valve from March 1925.

Until May 1932 it had a boiler with a Schmidt superheater and with handholes for washout purposes. For braking, it was dual fitted and acquired the usual swan-neck standpipe for the front end vacuum connection.

In July 1932 it was fitted with a newly built boiler with a Robinson superheater and which had five plugs at each side instead of handholes. Sight screens were fitted on the cab, and it got GS buffers and draw hook. The Westinghouse pump and piping were taken off and the engine became steam braked. The two handle steam reversing gear was retained. It went to works on 21st November 1934, to Darlington, its five previous general repairs having been at Gateshead works, which had been closed in January 1933. Needing new cylinders, it was decided to rebuild it with rotary cam Lentz valves.

The final development of C7 class was the rebuilding of No.732 with 17in. cylinders and Lentz poppet valves as used by the D49 Hunt class. This took place between 21st February and 21st December 1933. Screw reverse took over from steam and gave the opportunity to change to left hand driving position. Note also the switching of the whistles, and the new style cab. A normal boiler (a 1922 build) was used but the smokebox length was increased from 5ft 0½in. to 6ft 3¾in. and a chimney with a lip all round supplanted a capuchon. Two Wakefield mechanical lubricators were driven from the leading crank pin and vacuum brake was put on the engine.

Other alterations at the 1933 rebuilding were the moving of the bogie twelve inches forward and fitting it with 3ft 1¼in. instead of 3ft 7 in. wheels but the wheelbase remained 6ft 6in. The tender was changed to that with the extended rails from No.2202 which 732 then kept to its December 1946 withdrawal. In April 1938 the November 1936 built boiler shown here was fitted - note this batch had handholes and not plugs for washing out. The twin whistles were taken off and replaced by a single whistle mounted on top of an isolating valve.

In connection with the change to vacuum brake only on the engine and tender, two vacuum reservoirs were put on top of the tender behind the coal space. With the longer railed tender they were only noticeable from the rear.

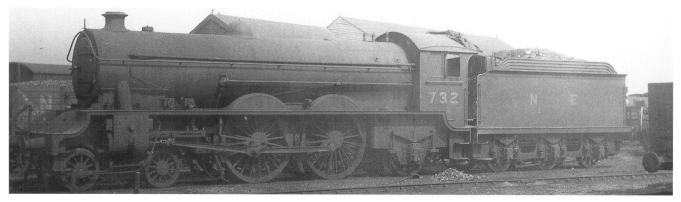

Repaired in October 1940, No.732 retained green painting until it went to works on 28th March 1944. It was ex works on 6th May 1944 in unlined black and with only NE on its tender. It arrived in works on 14th November 1946 having been renumbered 2963 only four days previously at Scarborough shed, but was not repaired and it was withdrawn on 14th December, the engine being cut up by 28th December 1946 and the boiler by 8th February 1947. The tender then went to new B1 class No.1038 in December 1947.

With the 'Uniflow' engine No.2212 needing new cylinders when it went for repair in November 1934, the choice was either to scrap or rebuild. The latter was the outcome and whilst outwardly the same as No.732, No.2212 got the improved Lentz gear with seven cam positions instead of the five on No.732. It also got 7in instead of $6^5/_{16}$in. exhaust valves. When ex works as Part 2 on 14th January 1936 the brake had been changed from steam to vacuum.

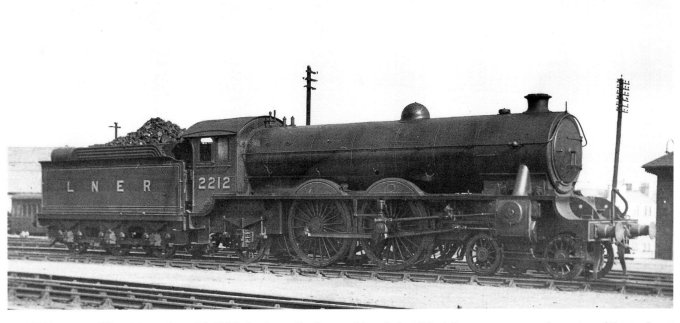

No.2212's tender differed from that with 732 in having rails of normal length, but it had the vacuum reservoirs on top of the tender at the rear. On 5th May 1942 it had a change of boiler to one built in 1928 but it was not recorded as changing from the twin whistles which it kept at its rebuilding. Also in May 1942 it was painted unlined black but still with LNER on the tender and although allocated 2997 it was not renumbered as it was withdrawn on 16th October 1945. The engine and boiler were cut up by 1st December 1945 but the tender remained spare until cut up in August 1948.

CLASS C 8

730

Gateshead 45.

To traffic 4/1906.

REPAIRS:
???. ?/?—?/3/15.**G.**
Ghd. 8/12/22—1/2/23.**L.**
Ghd. 19/1—9/6/25.**G.**
Ghd. 3—9/12/25.**L.**
Ghd. 20/7—6/8/26.**L.**
Ghd. 30/11/26—17/1/27.**L.**
Dar. 19/8/27—9/1/28.**G.**
Ghd. 12/4—8/5/28.**L.**
Dar. 20/11/28—16/1/29.**L.**

Ghd. 24—28/1/29.**N/C.**
Ghd. 19—28/3/29.**L.**
Ghd. 2/4—7/6/30.**G.**
Dar. 2/1/35. *Not repaired.*

BOILERS:
G490.
D420 *(new, sup.)* ?/3/15.

SHEDS:
Gateshead.
Heaton 24/11/33.

CONDEMNED: 4/1/35.
Cut up at Darlington.

731

Gateshead 46.

To traffic 5/1906.

REPAIRS:
???. ?/?—?/3/15.**G.**
Ghd. 22/6—1/11/23.**G.**
Ghd. 11/6—13/8/26.**L.**
Ghd. 5/8—7/10/27.**L.**
Ghd. 15/11/28—22/2/29.**G.**
Ghd. 12/3—2/4/30.**L.**
Ghd. 8/4—12/5/32.**L.**
Dar. 13—22/2/33.**N/C.**
Dar. 28/12/33. *Not repaired.*

BOILERS:
G492.
D413 *(new, sup.)* ?/3/15.

SHEDS:
Gateshead.
Heaton 24/11/33.

CONDEMNED: 28/12/33.
Cut up at Darlington.

(opposite, top) **In Darlington for general repair, and ex works on 9th January 1928, No.730 had changed its smokebox door fastening from a wheel and handle to two handles. Note the tender just had three rails all round and never had the usual extra rail around the coal space. Schmidt type superheater was used and the handwheel steam control for protecting the elements was retained.**

(opposite, centre) **Used almost throughout its life on the main line between York and Edinburgh, dual brakes were fitted and kept to withdrawal. Until January 1929 the front-end connections were below the buffer beam but in that month No.730 got a swan-neck vacuum standpipe (*see* page 105, bottom). Note Class 4.C.C. on the buffer beam; Class C8 was never carried, nor were cab side screens fitted.**

(opposite, bottom) **The other engine No.731, built in May 1906, differed in having Walschaerts gear for the valves. This was not apparent because both engines only had two sets of valve motion and this was between the frames. This engine also got a new boiler with a Schmidt superheater in March 1915 and never had the Gresley anti-vacuum valve fitted. Niddrie.**

Until at least 1927, No.731 had twin handles on its smokebox door but then changed to a wheel and handle which it kept to withdrawal. Ex Gateshead on 22nd February 1929, it had a swan-neck vacuum standpipe and had also been changed to Group Standard buffers and drawhook.

No.731 was dual braked also and kept the Westinghouse pump and piping to withdrawal. Both engines were unusual in having dual brakes on their tender.

Both had fully lined NER green livery at Grouping with a large armorial on the tender and the smaller circular version on the rear splasher. No.731 (*see* page 86, bottom) was ex Gateshead on 1st November 1923 in LNER green and with area suffix D. No.730 kept the NER livery until it went to works on 19th January 1925 and its new LNER livery dated from 9th June 1925.

No.731, ex Gateshead on 22nd February 1929, was just too early to have the number moved to the cab and as that was its last major repair, it kept the number on its tender to its 28th December 1933 withdrawal.

No.730 was ex Gateshead on 7th June 1930 with the number moved to the cab side, and with 12in. LNER on its tender. Note that it retained NER buffers and drawhook, and that was its last repair before withdrawal on 4th January 1935. Darlington, 1932.

CLASS C 9

727

Darlington - Rebuilt
from Class C7.

To traffic 16/11/31.

REPAIRS:
Dar. 23/1—16/11/31.*Rebuilt.*
Shop grey & C7 on bufferbeam.
Dar. 14—23/12/31.**N/C.**
Painted only.
Dar. 16—25/2/32.**N/C.**
Dar. 28/4—13/5/32.**L.**
Dar. 6/9—28/12/32.**L.**
Dar. 17/5—14/7/33.**L.**
Dar. 29/11/33—31/1/34.**G.**
Dar. 16—20/4/34.**N/C.**
Dar. 20/6—22/8/36.**L.**
Dar. 8/1—4/2/37.**L.**
Booster removed.

Dar. 24/8—29/10/37.**G.**
Dar. 1—3/11/37.**N/C.**
Dar. 26/6—19/10/39.**L.**
Dar. 13/2—18/4/41.**G.**
Dar. 21—25/4/41.**N/C.**
Dar. 8—26/1/42.**L.**
Dar. 26/3—9/4/42.**N/C.**
Dar. 29/12/42. *Not repaired.*

BOILER:
2415 *(new)* 16/11/31.

SHEDS:
York.
Gateshead 3/12/31.
Tweedmouth 19/8/39.
Heaton 2/11/40.

CONDEMNED: 23/1/43.
Cut up at Darlington.

2171

Darlington - Rebuilt
from Class C7.

To traffic 7/12/31.

REPAIRS:
Dar. 9/2—7/12/31.*Rebuilt.*
Dar. 2—9/2/32.**N/C.**
C9 put on bufferbeam.
Dar. 22/3—31/3/32.**N/C.**
Dar. 12—28/7/32.**L.**
Dar. 2—3/8/32.**N/C.**
Dar. 25/8/32—16/1/33.**L.**
LH tender bogie frame cracked.
Dar. 16—22/8/33.**N/C.**
Dar. 20/9—25/9/33.**N/C.**
Dar. 8/1—23/2/34.**G.**
Booster taken off.

Dar. 4/2—4/4/35.**L.**
Booster re-fitted.
Dar. 30/11—31/12/36.**N/C.**
Booster removed.
Dar. 23/4—30/9/37.**G.**
Dar. 18/8—5/10/38.**N/C.**
Dar. 2/8—6/9/39.**L.**
Dar. 19/2/42. *Not repaired.*

BOILER:
2416 *(new)* 7/12/31.

SHEDS:
Gateshead.
Tweedmouth 27/5/39.
Heaton 2/11/40.

CONDEMNED: 25/4/42.
Cut up at Darlington.

(opposite, top) **The driving position was changed to the left-hand side and rather curiously the steam reversing gear was retained although with single handle control. As early as 16th to 25th February 1932, it was in works for sight screens to be fitted on the cab. As the new boiler was pitched 1in. higher, no capuchon was provided, nor did the safety valves have a cover at their base. The front buffer beam was now a single plate and not a sandwich.**

(opposite, centre) **From 17th May to 14th July 1933, No.727 was in Darlington for a new axle to be fitted on the booster bogie, otherwise that engine had no serious troubles, but additions to Class A3 and the easy way in which A4 No.2511 tackled Cockburnspath Bank showed booster fitting had been successfully developed too late and overtaken by other events. This 1931 boiler saw the introduction of a single whistle mounted above an isolating valve. The Raven fog-signalling striker can just be discerned in front of the trailing coupled wheels, but this apparatus was removed when shopped on 29th November 1933 to 31st January 1934 for a general repair. Darlington, June 1933.**

(opposite, bottom) **In December 1936 it was decided to dispense with boosters and from 8th January to 4th February 1937, No.727 was in shops for the booster and associated pipes to be removed. The extra sandboxes serving the booster were also taken off but the exhaust steam injector was retained. The rocking grate mechanism put on at rebuilding can now be seen clearly. Note that the wheel on the smokebox door has now been replaced by a second handle.**

Later minor additions were the drain from the vacuum ejector exhaust and the ARP screen. As No.727's last general repair was 18th April 1941 it retained the green livery to its withdrawal on 23rd January 1943.

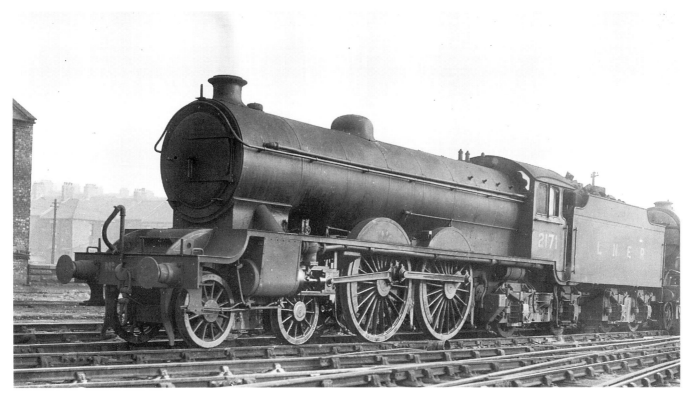

No.2171 underwent parallel rebuilding to No.727 from 9th February to 7th December 1931. They must have had their smokebox doors exchanged because 2171 went in with a wheel and handle type but came out with two handles whereas No.727 took two handles in but had a wheel and a handle when it came out. Details were the same for both engines in all other respects.

On both engines, at rebuilding, an exhaust steam injector was fitted and as it could not be placed in the usual position under the cab, it was fitted below the boiler barrel. The water control was a horizontal rod from the cab to a bevel gear box with another rod down to the water inlet valve. Ahead of the gearbox was a combined steam and delivery valve with the steam control rod passing through the boiler handrail. The overflow pipe curled round the front of the rear coupled wheel.

The booster on No.2171 was the cause of frequent trouble. From 25th August 1932 to 16th January 1933 the engine was out of traffic due to the tender rear bogie having a cracked frame. From a general repair on 23rd February 1934 it came out with the booster removed and was in again on 4th February to 4th April 1935 for the booster to be refitted.

No.2171 on 5th May 1935 after the booster had been refitted. Note the overflow pipe from the exhaust steam injector curling round the rear coupled wheel. Gateshead, 5th May 1935.

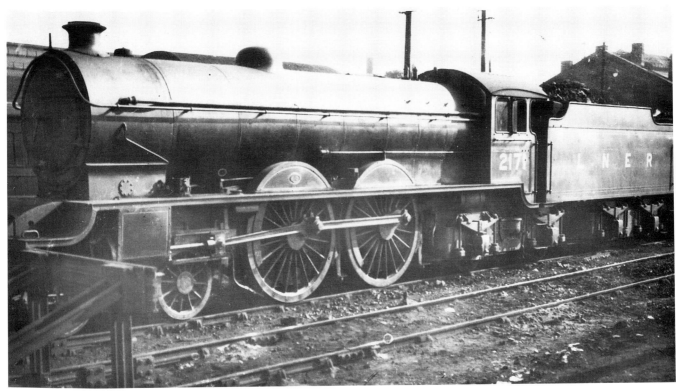

No.2171 was in works again from 30th November to 31st December 1936 for removal of the booster and its associated equipment. Note blanking-off plate on the smokebox saddle and that a drainpipe for vacuum ejector exhaust has now been fitted.

No.2171's last general repair and painting was from 23rd April to 30th September 1937, so it retained green livery to withdrawal on 25th April 1942. The engine was cut up on 6th June 1942 and the boiler on 9th October 1943 as it was not useable on another class. The tenders from both were later rebuilt to conventional form and used by B1's Nos.1038 and 1039. Gateshead shed, 15th April 1938.